Contents

Editorial

'Victims [of violence against women] are chosen because of their gender. The message is domination: stay in your place or be afraid. Contrary to the argument that such violence is only personal or cultural, it is profoundly political.' (Bunch and Carrillo 1992)

On the occasion of the 50th anniversary of the UN Declaration of Human Rights in November 1998, many organisations working on gender and women's issues are choosing to highlight, once again, the endemic violence against women which continues to exist in countries throughout the world. The extent of this violence can be seen in the statistics: the World Health Organisation estimates that at least one in five women has been physically or sexually abused by a man or men at some time in her life (WHO, 1997), and according to a study by the World Bank drawing on data from 35 countries, one-quarter to more than half of women report having been physically abused by a present or former partner, while far more have suffered emotional and psychological abuse (Heise 1994). Mindful of statistics like these, this collection of articles focuses specifically on violence against women, rather than more widely on violence and gender, which would have permitted an examination of violence against men and boys.

Violence has been usefully defined as 'any action or structure that diminishes another human being' (Pinthus 1982, 2, in Ramazanoglu 1987). However, the limited space available prohibits comprehensive coverage of the many different forms of abuse experienced by women which could be embraced by this definition. Issues which *are* addressed here include female genital mutilation, early marriage, abuse and beatings within the home, and rape and sexual assault — by partners, acquaintances or strangers, in 'formal' armed conflict and as racist violence against minorities. Writers in this collection look at violence against women in many different settings: in conflict and in peacetime; in the home and in public; as members of 'different' ethnic groupings; as children and as adults. While most articles concentrate on one specific manifestation of violence against women, Noeleen Heyzer of UNIFEM provides an overview in hers of the many forms of violence against women throughout the world, and outlines strategies to combat this. Purna Sen also takes a broad perspective on violence, from the angle of development practice and policy.

Researching the causes of male violence

Cross-cultural research suggests 'the existence of "male" violence against women in all societies and across time' (Dobash and Dobash 1998, forthcoming). It is found in every socio-economic group, ideology, class, race, and ethnic grouping. 'If violence [were] a form of random deviance rather than a reflection of recurring social relations, then one need not worry about the shape and form of everyday social life, but only about deviations from it' (ibid). In line with this, in her article on the work of Sakshi, a 'violence intervention centre' in India, Aanchal Kapur argues that until a transformation of 'everyday' gender relations occurs, men's violence cannot be ended at its source, because it is rooted in unequal relations of power between men and women, and women's resistance to that control (Pickup, 1998). In this sense at least, there is a structural explanation for all male violence against women — the existence of patriarchy. 'Patriarchy, or the sex/gender order, has at its disposal a whole range of techniques and mechanisms of control. Among these are force and physical violence.' (Edwards 1987, 24)

However, differences in the form and pattern of male violence against women in different societies does give hope that social policy and practice can lessen or end such violence. Variation in 'both the nature and level of this violence between men and across different societies and/or cultural contexts... suggests cultural specificity and the importance of different contexts rather than an unvaried, universal behaviour' (Dobash and Dobash 1998, forthcoming). Determining what circumstances aggravate societal violence is therefore the first step in much research by social policy and development institutions.

In her article on pornography and violence against women, Teboho Maitse explores different poverty- and militarisation-based explanations for widespread male violence against women in South Africa, which continues in the post-apartheid era. Maitse argues that explanations of male violence which focus on disadvantage, or even violence, in society are dangerous if, as a result, attention is taken away from the

fact that individual men are free agents who can choose to use or reject violent behaviour, whatever the social conditions. Theories of violence which attribute male violence to social causes may encourage policymakers to condone male abuse, and fail to challenge the general societal apathy which surrounds men's violence against women. Such theories have been advanced by various organisations including the UN, which has described violence as a way of life in situations of poor housing and economic vulnerability (UN 1989).

In her article on Oxfam's research into domestic violence in Eastern Europe, Sarah Maguire considers the links between armed conflict, the militarisation of society, and violence against women in the home. She argues that a direct relationship between increased violence in wider society and increased male violence cannot be assumed — in her research, findings were far more complex and contradictory.

The concerns raised by Maguire and Maitse are shared by other researchers into male violence, who assert that social research must be conducted responsibly, because it cannot be separated from its political, cultural, and moral contexts. Jeff Hearn, a researcher into 'men's violences', points out that research which focuses on men and their experiences of 'masculinity' in the absence of a feminist awareness of gender power relations may actually entrench the status quo, by being 'all too appealing [to men] as a means to further power' (Hearn 1998,1). Funding and other resources for research into male perpretrators of violence, and for rehabilitation work with them, should not be seen as an alternative to working with women who have been victims of male violence, but as a complementary strategy.

Violence and choice

Women experience violence in different forms, depending, among other factors, on their age and social position. Two articles in this collection address different facets of young women's experience of violence. Mariam Ouattara, Purna Sen, and Marilyn Thomson discuss different experiences of early marriage in Africa and Asia. Joan Cameron and Karen Rawlings Anderson discuss female genital mutilation (FGM) among Somali women who have migrated to Britain, and draw a parallel between reasons given for its continuation with reasons given by British health practitioners to justify the practice of episiotomy during childbirth. While both early marriage and FGM are acknowledged by feminist activists and practitioners in gender and development work as a clear example of a fundamental abuse of the rights of girl children and of women, these forms of violence continue to exist because a complex web of economic and social factors limits women's choices.

Conceptualising violence against women in this way, as the ultimate outcome of a profound lack of choices open to women and girls, should convince development agencies to see the desperate need for them to address the issue. Understanding violence as the outcome of a lack of choices also enables us to understand why girls or women who are the victims of family violence often choose to survive it by staying in the relationship where the abuse has taken place, rather than by challenging the abuse; it also helps to explain why older women mete out violent practices on girls in their care (Kandiyoti 1988; 1998). There are meagre economic and social resources available to women who abandon codes of conformity in male-dominated societies. While men have autonomy to reject violence as an option, women are typically faced not only with economic barriers which prevent them from leaving abusive men, but also with a barrage of opposition on grounds of culture and social norms.

Development and violence against women

Violence against women has only relatively recently been widely acknowledged to be a key issue for development and social policy. Purna Sen identifies three main approaches to violence against women from a development perspective. First, such violence impedes the efficiency or effectiveness of development interventions; second, it is the ultimate obstacle to women's full and equal participation in social, economic, and political activities; and third, it is an offence against all notions of universal human rights. Sen identifies three variants within this human-rights approach: principles of human rights, rights to bodily integrity, and the UNDP's view of human development as being related to the 'enlargement of choices'.

Human rights and international responses

Human-rights perspectives on violence against women not only stress the need to change international and national legal systems, but also the need for these to be held accountable for failures to enforce laws set up to protect women (Cook 1995). In addition, cultural change must take place — laws alone cannot protect women from male violence. In particular, it is essential to make the links between violence against women in the home and in public, in conflict and in times of relative stability. In her article, Noeleen Heyzer charts the development of a concern for violence against women in the UN system, and outlines the current UNIFEM campaign to eradicate such violence. She stresses the need for a holistic strategy which uses not only legal mechanisms, but also mass campaigning action on the part of local communities and development NGOs. Galuh Wandita's article offers an example of women campaigning against violence, through collecting evidence and testimonies for use at national, as well as international, levels.

The article focuses on the recent riots in Indonesia, in which Chinese Indonesian women were the primary target of mass rapes and sexual violence.

Challenging the idea of a 'private sphere'

While work on violence against women in conflict and in the public sphere, informed by a human-rights perspective, is taking place, organisational attitudes to working on the issue of violence against women which takes place in the 'private sphere' of the home are particularly resistant to change. Despite this, women are statistically safer in the street than they are in their homes (Winters et al, 1998). Many cultures have considered the marital relationship in particular, and the family more generally, as a private area, in which others should not interfere with the freedom of the male household head to control events and decisions, and punish challenges to his authority.

This profound unease with 'interfering' in the 'private sphere' of the home has been carried over into ideals of bureaucracies, which have shaped common-sense ideas of what organisations should be (Gender and Development Vol 5 No 1). It is shared by institutions including the police and the judiciary, as well as by development organisations. Even in countries where gender-based violence is recognised as a crime, only a small proportion of survivors of male violence report these crimes to police. Tanya Lipovskaya, of the Sisters Sexual Assault Recovery Centre, confirms the results of this institutional bias against women: in Moscow, Russia, the police reject complaints of sexual violence from married woman and single women who have been sexually active. In her article, Aanchal Kapur discusses work which Sakshi, an NGO in India, has carried out to challenge such attitudes. Ironically, while the support of development organisations is needed to enable such work to be funded, Kapur points out that interventions which are long-term and concerned with cultural change are incompatible with donors' demands to see tangible results.

The cost of violence to development

One pragmatic way of persuading development organisations to fund work which challenges violence against women by promoting cultural change and support for the survivors of violence is to demonstrate the *negative* impact that it has on women. 'Domestic' violence hampers women from using their skills in development activities, and carries costs to them, their families, and society which are incalculable (Heise 1994). The World Bank estimates that the wider category of 'gender-based victimisation' is responsible for one out of every five healthy days of life lost to women or reproductive age (World Bank 1993, quoted in Heise 1994, 78). While this efficiency-based approach to combating violence may be distasteful to feminist activists who are struggling to have violence recognised as a human-rights issue, there is ample evidence to support the argument.

Increased violence as a response to women's 'empowerment'

The connections between women's participation in development activities, the challenges these offer to gender power relations, and potential increases in male violence in the household, are the focus of much current debate (for example, Kabeer 1998 in the context of credit interventions). While the links between participation, 'empowerment' of women, and male violence are complex, there is evidence that violence against women increases in intensity where gender relations are being transformed and male privilege is challenged (Rowlands 1997).

In times of family need, women's role as economic providers for their families can oblige them to challenge gender stereotypes, by entering socially unacceptable situations in order to earn a living. In these situations, they are especially vulnerable to male violence. This is especially true of women who migrate to cities or wealthy countries, those who work as domestic or sex workers, women in prostitution, and refugee women collecting humanitarian assistance in areas of a camp where women are known to be raped (Gender and Development Vol 6 No 1, 1998).

Development organisations must recognise the existence of male violence against women as a barrier to development, and integrate this reality into their planning, to ensure that development interventions do not place women at risk of increased violence. They must also support those who face it (Schuler et al., 1998). This not only means providing the fullest possible information on possible outcomes of a planned project, and allowing women to decide freely whether they wish to take part in it. It also means exploring how women's existing mutual support systems could be strengthened or augmented in order to enable them to deal with an increased risk of male violence. In many contexts, women themselves — individually, collectively, and in organsations — have developed complex strategies to prevent violence (Levinson 1989). To do this effectively, development workers must address their own prejudices about male violence against women, its relevance to development, and its legitimacy as an issue which development organisations must confront if their work is to benefit women.

References

Bunch C and Carrillo R (1992) *Gender Violence: a development and human rights issue*, UNIFEM.

Cook R (1995) 'Enforcing Women's Rights Through Law', *Gender and Development* Vol 3 No 1, Oxford, Oxfam UK.

Dobash R Emerson and Dobash RP (1998) 'Introduction', in Dobash R Emerson and Dobash RP (eds), *Rethinking Violence Against Women*, Sage, UK.

Edwards A (1987) 'Male Violence in Feminist Theory: an Analysis of the Changing Conceptions of Sex/Gender Violence and Male Dominance', in Hamner J and Maynard M (eds), *Women, Violence and Social Control*, Macmillan, UK.

Gender and Development on Organisational Culture, Vol 5 No 1, 1997, Oxfam, UK.

Hearn J (1998) *The Violences of Men*, Sage, UK.

Heise L (1994) 'Overcoming violence: a background paper on violence against women as an obstacle to development', in Reardon G (ed), *Power and Process: a report from the Women Linking for Change Conference*, Oxfam, UK.

Kabeer N, (1998) *'Money Can't Buy Me Love'? Evaluating Gender, Credit and Empowerment in Rural Bangladesh*, IDS Discussion Paper 363, University of Sussex, UK.

Kandiyoti D, 'Bargaining with Patriarchy', in *Gender and Society*, Vol 2 No 3, 1988.

Pickup F (1998) Background Concept Paper for Oxfam staff conference on Violence Against Women, unpublished (publication forthcoming 1999, Oxfam, UK).

Ramazanoglu C (1987) 'Sex and Violence in Academic Life, or You Can Keep a Good Woman Down', in Hamner J and Maynard M (eds.), *Women, Violence and Social Control*, Macmillan, UK.

Rowlands J (1997) *Questioning Empowerment: Working with Women in Honduras*, Oxfam, UK.

Schuler SR, Hashemi SM, and Badal SH, (1998) 'Men's violence against women in rural Bangladesh: undermined or exarcerbated by microcredit programmes?', *Development in Practice*, Vol 8 No 2, Oxfam, UK.

United Nations (1989) *Violence Against Women in the Family*.

Winters M et al (1998) 'Violence Against Women' in *Our Bodies, Ourselves for the New Century*, Touchstone (Simon and Schuster Inc), USA.

World Health Organisation (1997) *Violence Against Women*.

Development practice and violence against women

Purna Sen

Development practitioners and organisations are increasingly addressing violence against women, partly because it is seen to hinder development — constraining the efficiency of projects, limiting women's particpation, and denying them their human rights. However, it is wrong to simply portray gender-based violence as an aspect of underdevelopment, Sen argues, and stresses the need for strong, visible local support networks for women.

Rape, domestic violence, trafficking, sexual abuse, incest, female infanticide, prostitution, genital mutilation — there are so many ways in which women experience violence. Awareness of this seems to be growing in many fields, including development discourse, which has recently begun to pay attention to violence against women, both within mainstream development, and in the field of gender and development. Development literature which addresses violence against women tends to take one of three approaches. While the first of these argues that violence against women limits the effectiveness or efficiency of development projects, the second focuses on how such violence hinders participation, and the third argues that violence is an offence against human development, and all forms of economic development must address the issue. I will discuss these perspectives after commenting briefly on the nature and extent of violence against women and discussing some examples. I then go on to indicate practical ways in which violence against women can be addressed in development. Finally, I make some suggestions

as to how women can be enabled to contest violence, and how development organisations can foster a social attitude of intolerance towards such abuse.

I would like to start, however, by clarifying why I focus on violence against women and the role of men as perpetrators. Increasingly, voices are raised querying this focus. Objections are raised concerning the identity of perpetrators and victims of violence, arguing that women abuse women, and that men are also victims of interpersonal violence. Constraints of space prohibit me from discussing these arguments at length, so it must suffice to observe a few facts. To start with, both qualitative and quantitative research repeatedly show that the vast majority of violence experienced by women is at the hands of men — largely of men known to the victims — and assaults often occur within the home (Bachman and Saltzman 1995; Butchart, Lerer, and Blanche 1994). It is indeed true that men experience violence from others — but, as with women, this is mostly at the hands of other men. It is also known that women can and do use violence; this is no less unacceptable than when men use violence. Women from south Asia, for example, have long drawn attention to the unfavourable power dynamics in a new bride's marital home, which may involve violence inflicted by senior females. (While little of this research has found its way into published literature, references include Calman 1992.) In addition, the casework of activists and campaigners include many examples of mother-in-law violence; recently, a south Asian woman living in London, UK, successfully had her mother-in-law charged for abusing and imprisoning her, resulting in a prison sentence (see Sen 1998 for a brief discussion of this case, handled by Southall Black Sisters).

The use and meaning of violence is connected with power. It is broadly the case that in most societies, social, economic, political, and interpersonal power remains with men: power is socially gendered. In this context, violence is an expression of power, a means through which people seek control (as the examples below illustrate), and a gendered practice. This is not to say that women's violence should be ignored — in fact, all violence should be abhorred and addressed. But in this article, in recognition of the gendered and widespread nature of violence against women, I shall concentrate on male violence.

The nature and extent of violence against women

Women across all regions, ages, religions, classes, and political affiliations are vulnerable to violence; their safety is guaranteed neither in the home nor in public spaces. Personal accounts from numerous countries show the nature and impact of violence against women, and these accounts are slowly being supplemented by systematic research on these aspects, as well as by research on incidence and prevalence.

While developing countries are increasingly providing this kind of information, until recently little research on violence against women has been available; our knowledge of some aspects, such as prevalence, is limited. Police records are sometimes used to estimate the extent of violence against women, and to support arguments that rapid neo-liberal economic restructuring or other forms of 'modernisation' have accompanied increases in the level of violence against women (eg Womankind 1990; Bradley 1994). However, evidence suggests that police statistics are likely to significantly underestimate the true extent of violence. The small body of specific national surveys on violence against women indicate that actual levels of violence are considerable — for example, a national survey by the Law Reform Commission in Papua New Guinea discovered that 67 per cent of women in rural areas and 56 per cent of women in urban areas had been abused by their husbands (Bradley 1994). In Brazil in 1985, over 70 per cent of all cases of violence against women reported to the Sao Paulo police occurred within the home (Thomas 1994), while in Costa Rica, it was found that 95 per cent of pregnant girls under 16 years of age were victims of incest (UNIFEM 1992). In India during the 1980s, registered cases of 'dowry deaths' (excluding suicides and accidents) grew from 990 in 1985 to 1,790 in the first ten months of 1987 (Calman 1992). A Tanzanian survey found that 90 per cent of employed women said that sexual harassment threatens their jobs and 100 per cent of housewives said they had been sexually harassed in the streets (Tanzania Media Women's Association 1994).

These figures are in line with research from countries in economic transition: in Russia, police figures indicate that 14,500 women die each year due to domestic violence (Family Violence Prevention Fund 1997). The picture is similar in industrialised contexts: for example, 51 per cent of women in Canada have experienced some form of violence in their adult lives

(Johnson 1996), and an average of 75 women are killed each year by their husbands. For each woman so killed, 2,250 women experience violence at the hands of their male partners (Wilson, Johnson and Daly 1995).

While statistics such as these indicate the extent of violence, individual accounts show us the nature of violence and how it impacts on women's lives. These accounts expose the horror of violence, and the similarities which exist between ostensibly different forms of violence, and between situations in which violence occurs. For instance, it appears that women experience violence and torture both in situations of conflict and where there is no 'formal' conflict (i.e. where there is no breakdown of public peace or social institutions).

Domestic and political violence can take much the same form. Torture of women political prisoners in Latin America has involved various forms of sexual violence as well as rape: '[C]igarettes are extinguished on the woman's breasts and nipples; her breasts are slashed with sharpened instruments; blades, hot irons and electrical surgical pens are used to brand different parts of her body' (Bunster-Burotto 1994, 168).

During my own research on domestic violence one woman told me of sexual abuse akin to torture in her marriage: 'At night, one time, he tied my bangles together so there would be no noise for anyone to hear when he came to do his work... [Another time] he bit my breasts and left sores on my skin... one time he used his toenail to cut the skin around my vagina' (Sen 1997, 151). The incidence of acid attacks appears to be increasing in Bangladesh (Naripokkho). Men throw acid at (often young) girls who refuse to conform to their demands, either by rejecting or ignoring their attentions. Men often aim at women's heads and faces so that their resulting disfigurement is visible to all, their marriage prospects are effectively destroyed, and their entire families are shamed and dishonoured. It is difficult for victims of acid attacks to return to school to face their peers, and to move around in public places. The impact of such attacks should be compared with the mild consequences for the assailants: out of 80 cases known to have taken place in Bangladesh in 1996, only two ended in criminal convictions (Huq, 5 August 1998).

In Papua New Guinea, gang rapes of women travelling in public spaces are a matter of great concern (Robie 1997); in one recent assault, a woman was abducted by a bus driver and his accomplice and suffered a night-long ordeal of rape by more than 20 men. The absence of safety for women in the streets curtails women's movements and actions. How can women who want or are invited to participate in projects do so if they fear for their safety in public spaces (including public transport)? How can women be productive at work if they are beaten and raped at home, and suffer not only the attacks but also the stress of constantly concealing this reality and their responses? The implications for women's participation which can be drawn from these examples are relevant beyond the countries in which they take place.

Development frameworks and violence

As stated at the start of this article, there are three main approaches to violence against women in development research and practice.

An impediment to efficiency or effectiveness

In an efficiency approach, women are seen primarily as a resource for development, rather than beneficiaries (Moser 1989). Since women form (approximately) half of any national population, an efficient development project must tap their capacities in order to make optimal use of resources.

An efficiency argument focusing on violence considers that violated women are a wasted resource, particularly because their participation labour force is constrained, or that the economic costs of violence against women are unacceptable. The World Bank has recognised that violence against women presents a problem, and calculates that rape and domestic violence 'account for about 5 per cent of the total disease burden among women aged 15-44 in developing countries' (World Bank 1993:50). This focus sees good health as a necessary instrument to 'provide a foundation for future economic growth' (World Bank 1993:52). For economic growth to be effective, women must enjoy good health, which violence places in jeopardy.

Another respect in which violence can be seen to result in inefficient use of a nation's resources is through the direct and indirect financial costs incurred both by individuals and the state. These costs include lost days at work, lost earnings, increased health-care demand, emergency housing costs, a need for child guidance, counselling, psychiatric, and legal services, as well as the involvement of police and penal institutions. Not all of these are relevant in all contexts, but a common core will include costs to the police service, the health-care services, lost workdays, and lost earnings.

Few attempts have been made to quantify these costs. A study in New South Wales, Australia, estimated that violence against women incurred costs of more than Aus$1,500 million per year, using 1990 figures (National Committee on Violence Against Women 1993). These are conservative estimates, because ripple and multiplier effects may drive up the overall cost. The criminal-justice system of New York City alone is estimated to have spent US$41 million (for police court and prison costs) in 1989 on processing cases following domestic violence arrests (Zorza 1994). The Inter-American Development Bank has

estimated that in 1996, domestic violence resulted in the loss of 2 per cent of GDP in Chile and of 1.6 per cent in Nicaragua, through the loss of women's wages alone (reported by Family Violence Prevention Fund 1997).

Where efficiency and effectiveness are watchwords of development projects and programmes, violence against women has a considerable and direct detrimental impact. The costs of violence are borne not only by the women or children affected, but also by wider society and the public services.

An obstacle or barrier to participation

Actual and threatened violence has impeded women's participation in development projects. Many development initiatives include or encourage the participation of women, typically assuming that women's labour can be harnessed without cost, and that they have almost limitless free time (Moser 1989). Participation itself is seen as a 'good thing', an objective in itself, which must be sought in all kinds of development activity. This perspective is closely connected to ways of thinking — often based on principles of equity or justice — in which people are seen as active partners, who bring something of value to development processes and perhaps gain something for themselves.

Participation is a central tenet of much contemporary development work, but it needs to be problematised, not only in terms of the gendered difficulties of engaging in various activities (for example, where women are customarily confined to the home it is difficult to build successful projects which centre on women's activities in other spaces) but also in terms of violence. While the development community has come to realise that problems such as high fertility, deforestation, and hunger cannot be solved without women's full participation, women cannot contribute their work or creative ideas fully when they are burdened with the physical and psychological scars of violence (Heise 1989). Where women are encouraged, by development agencies or by the state, to participate in income-generating activities, their movements in public spaces may be constrained as a result of their husbands' threats.

As Heise points out, violence limits women's ability to engage effectively or fully in development activities. But further, women's engagement in such activities may even precipitate violence at home (Sen 1997). Increased activity outside the home, activity in mixed company, or women's acquisition of a separate income may trigger bouts of domestic violence.

Violence as a contradiction to human development

The importance of people as beneficiaries of development, not only as the means to an end, is increasingly recognised. I will identify three variations within this approach: human rights, bodily integrity, and the UNDP's view of human development as being related to the 'enlargement of choices' (UNDP 1992, 2).

1. Human rights

Human rights have been argued to have a central relationship both to violence and development (Peters and Wolper 1995). In 1986, Georgina Ashworth provided a detailed analysis of the UN Declaration of Human Rights and how it can be read in relation to violence against women. She argued that the Charter failed women by not addressing and eliminating violence against them, which in effect denies women their human rights (Ashworth 1986). Worldwide agitation and lobbying on women's human rights have had considerable success in setting up mechanisms which have made violence a more central issue, such as the Convention on the Elimination of All Forms of Discrimination Against Women, adopted in 1979, and the appointment of a UN Special Rapporteur on Violence Against Women following the 1993 Vienna Conference on Human Rights.

The principle of universality which underlies human-rights frameworks has sparked off disagreement, particularly on the applicability of so-called Western notions of rights to Third-World countries which (it has been argued) have different, possibly more communitarian, approaches (for example, Mayer 1995). However, I would argue that the success of the human rights lobby is partly due to the fact that it does not separate out the developing from the developed world; this leads to an understanding that violence against women is a worldwide problem, and that the solution does not lie in Western experts bringing solutions to Southern women.

2. Bodily integrity

The second variation in the human-rights approach is associated with women's struggle to assert their 'reproductive rights', as distinct from the population and family-planning policies often delivered to women in the South. The attainment of reproductive rights is central to women's claim to autonomy, and has often clashed with development objectives and methods. For example, population policies in Malaysia, Singapore and China have been criticised for their instrumentalist treatment of women (Leng 1988; Davin 1991). Not only are women denied control of the functions and the use of their bodies, but many family planning programmes are insensitive even to women's health issues (Kabeer 1992).

It is not only the number of children a woman chooses to have, but also whether or not she chooses to have any, which are fundamental aspects of a woman's autonomy. Another relevant factor is her control over the conditions in which she makes these decisions, as 'we have not yet begun to formulate a social policy which affords women any kind of agency or subjectivity in carrying out her reproductive activities' (Pearson 1993, 5). Family-planning practices have involved bodily violations of women's reproductive rights, yet they lie at the heart of much development planning. Remarkably, the discourse on reproductive rights tends to omit discussion of sexual behaviour and sexual violence except, to some extent, in the discussion of HIV transmission.

3. Theories of human development

The third strand in this approach engages with theories of human development. Human development is defined as a concern with the enlargement of people's choices; it is a process which weaves development around people, not people around development (UNDP 1990-7). This formulation has the potential to include violence against women as a central issue, because violence contradicts the process of widening choices (Bunch and Carrillo 1992).

As mentioned in the introduction, violence against women is an expression of power by the abuser, and it often forms part of a range of control-seeking behaviours. It should be clear, then, that violence against women is in direct contradiction to women having control over their own lives, and to women's choices being widened. There is, implicitly, a mutual exclusivity — while there is violence against women, their choices are certainly not being widened.

For whom is violence an issue?

Alongside the increasing recognition of violence against women in development discourse, there seems to be a parallel increase in confusion about what can be done, and by whom. I shall use my work on domestic violence in Calcutta to draw out some issues, and to indicate the range of people who are in a position to intervene. I investigated women's resistance to

domestic violence in an Indian context (Sen 1997), and how it might be strengthened; in particular, I was interested in cases where women reported that violence had stopped. I found that there are three important contributors to the resolution of physical and sexual abuse in intimate relationships. The first is networks: contacts with family, neighbours, with women's organisations, and with legal advice centres. All these are associated with cessation of violent relationships. Networking is of central importance, both as a source of support and as a means of intervention during assaults, and to provide advice and employment opportunities for women who left or were left by abusive men. Women, and sometimes men, provided critical links between victims of violence and organisations which offered them support, and through which they could challenge men within relationships they wished to maintain, or through which they could plan to leave or take legal action.

Second, women's education beyond the primary level (as distinct from simply being literate) is very strongly associated with the cessation of violence. I found that no woman who had progressed beyond five years of formal education remained in a violent relationship. To put it more positively, women who had progressed beyond an elementary level of education had all moved on from violent relationships; all of them have either left or been left by violent men, and none continues to live with a man who ever abused her. Interestingly, they all had also forged positive relations with local women's groups. While these were not the only women who made the transition from violent to violence-free lives, analysis suggests that education may have a contributory role in enabling women to resist domestic violence. The achievement of universal primary education is of central importance for those interested in changing the current intolerable situations of violence against women. Much development interest in the education of girls tends to highlight the potential for increased worker productivity, the impact of education on fertility (such as a reduced fertility rate and better birth spacing), and the enhanced nutritional status of children. The impact of education on women's capacity to resist male violence has not been investigated before, but is of great significance. Girls need to be both encouraged and facilitated to complete and progress from primary education, and parents must be encouraged to support this.

Finally, women's employment is already a focus of much development work, but promoting it on its own may not 'empower' women — an aim which is of interest to many. I found that employment during a violent marriage was associated neither with resistance to violence nor a greater propensity to leave abusive men. However, employment emerged as significant in the foundation of independent lives (albeit often rather a limited one) for women who had separated from violent men. Thus, income-generating activities should take place in the context of facilitation of networking and education.

All three aspects — education, networking and employment — are of central relevance to development initiatives. Together these three factors form a basket of resources which I found to be of central importance in the resolution of domestic violence.

Ensuring development interventions support victims of violence

Awareness of the possibility that women are experiencing violence, and of their ability to respond, should be central to all development interventions, regardless of their focus or their target group. Women may be abused at home, at work, or during activities connected with the development intervention; they may be pregnant through force, caring for abused children, hungry, fearful of returning home, fearful of coming to work, or not in control of income which they receive. It is possible to work against violence with careful, considered, and sensitive approaches in which workers are alert to signs of violence and abuse (as women are reluctant to volunteer their experiences), perhaps as a result of training. Workers must also be clear that their organisation does not tolerate violence, perhaps in the context of organisational policies opposed to violence and in favour of challenging abuse. They also need to be as informed as possible on appropriate ways to respond to instances of abuse, involving training, networking with local opposition to violence, and keeping informed of local support services for abused women. These responses should be undertaken with due care, thought, and, if possible, with the help of training or at least consultation with those who have experience in working on gender-based violence.

Whether the target group in development projects is women only, mixed groups, or men only, it is possible to oppose violence. In women-only environments, participants may discuss violence; this provides an opening from which to express intolerance of abuse, offer support for victims, and pass on information on local support and advice services. Talking about rape, domestic violence or other abuse often brings shame, disapproval, dishonour, or blame on women, and interventions must avoid further victimisation of women whose secrets become known. It is important for women to be able to tell someone about what is happening to them, but development workers should not rush into a discussion without care and caution: women generally talk more readily to women whom they know — mothers, sisters, female friends or colleagues — and workers can put women in touch with local support workers.

In mixed groups, it is particularly important to be alert to the possibility of abuse of women. One woman in India told me about an incident when she was working in the fields and had to take a break to relieve herself. While she was alone during this break, she was sexually assaulted by a male worker. Work environments must become places where the safety of workers is assured, not where they are exposed to violence and abuse. In the company of men, whether in mixed or men-only groups, there must be an attitude of intolerance of violence and of other associated practices, and of ideologies and cultures of male dominance. It is for those who have access to male conversations to take the opportunities to challenge violence and supporting attitudes.

Where development actors engage with the state or state agencies, for example in capacity building or in training, the obligations of states to victims of violence should be borne in mind. In 1992, the Committee on the Elimination of All Forms of Discrimination Against Women (CEDAW) issued a recommendation that states take all actions necessary to protect women against violence.[1]

Conclusion

The most important starting point for action against violence against women is the recognition that it is neither exceptional nor acceptable. There is a danger in development work that violence against women can be seen as a correlate of underdevelopment or poverty. However, work which extends beyond a focus on poverty, and the similarities in women's experience of violence across the world, show clearly that women across income categories, in all countries, are subjected to male violence. The dominant risk factor is not poverty; it is being female. Culture or community should not be seen as limiting discussion of, action against, or opposition to violence. Cultural diversity is not the deciding factor in whether or not women experience violence, and it cannot be used to justify non-intervention. Culture also does not define whether or not violence against women is accepted or acceptable, just as culture does not determine whether or not economic exploitation, absolute poverty, or high infant mortality should be accepted. All violence must be seen to be unacceptable.

We need a significant change in thinking — research suggests that one in two (possibly more) women experience violence in their lives (for example, Johnson 1996 for Canada; Bradley 1994 for Papua New Guinea; Heise 1994 for various countries). Therefore, on average, every other woman with whom you come into contact has known or will know violence. If policy and practice start from this point, violence against women must be taken seriously, and seen as everyone's concern.

Policy approaches must recognise the endemic nature of violence against women, support research into prevalence and resistance, and recognise violence against women as based on unequal gender power relations. There are many ways in which development policy and practice can contribute to the reduction and elimination of violence against women, including a concern (and appropriate strategies and policies) for children from homes where violence against women is present. They may also be abused, or may witness horrific violence. Another concern should be challenging the behaviour of violent men, and their actions and talk of dominance and power over women. 'Zero tolerance' of violence impacts not only upon the way in which development workers engage with women victims of violence, but also how they deal with the male perpetrators. Consideration can be, but is rarely, given to sanctions against violent men.

The importance of linking women into local support-service networks cannot be over-emphasised. In their areas of work, these agencies always play a critical part in ensuring a social attitude of intolerance towards violence and in supporting individual women; development workers should keep informed about which organisations work in their areas, and which services they offer. However, most importantly, the capacity of local organisations to undertake the work they already do is severely limited by resource constraints. Perhaps two of the most important ways in which development policy-makers can seriously address the issue of violence against women, in the communities in which they work, is by strengthening these organisations both through funding and through consultation.

Purna Sen is a lecturer at the London School of Economics and researches violence against women both in the UK and elsewhere. She is an active member of Southall Black Sisters and CHANGE. Purna can be contacted at the Development Studies Institute, London School of Economics, Houghton Street, London WC2A 2AE, fax: 0171 955 6844, e-mail p.sen@lse.ac.uk.

Notes

1 These actions should include effective legal measures, penal sanctions, civil remedies, and compensatory provisions to protect women against all kinds of violence — including *inter alia* violence and abuse in the family, sexual assault and sexual harassment in the workplace — as well as preventive measures, such as public information and education programmes to change attitudes concerning the roles and status of men and women. States were instructed to establish protective measures, including refuge centres, counselling, rehabilitation and support services for women who are the victims of violence or who are at risk of violence. A significant aspect of CEDAW is making states liable for private acts of violence, and requiring them to eliminate gender discrimination by any person, organisation, or enterprise: 'States may also be responsible for private acts if they fail to act with due diligence to prevent violations of rights, or to investigate and punish acts of violence, and to provide compensation' (CEDAW 1992).

Bibliography

Ashworth, G (1986) *Of Violence And Violation and Human Rights*, London, Change.

Ashworth, G (1993) *Changing the Discourse: A Guide to Women and Human Rights*, London, Change Thinkbook.

Bachman, R and Saltzman, L E (1995) Violence Against Women: Estimates from the Redesigned Survey, US Department of Justice, Office of Justice Programs, Bureau of Justice Statistics.

Bradley, C (1994) 'Why Male Violence is a Development Issue: Reflections from Papua New Guinea' in Davies, M (ed) *Women and Violence: Realities and Responses Worldwide*, London, Zed.

Bunch, C and Carrillo, R (1992) *Gender Violence: a Development and Human Rights Issue*, Dublin, Attic Press.

Bunster-Burotto, X (1994) 'Surviving Beyond Fear: Women and Torture in Latin America', in Davies (ed) *Women and Violence: realities and responses worldwide*, pp 156–175.

Butchart, A, Lerer, L B and Blanche, M T (1994) 'Imaginary Constructions and Forensic Reconstructions of Fatal Violence Against Women — Implications for Community Violence Prevention' in *Forensic Science International*, Vol 64, No 1, pp 21–34.

Calman, L J (1992) *Toward Empowerment: Women and Movement Politics in India*, Oxford, Westview Press.

Davin, D (1991) 'Chinese Models of Development and Their Implications for Women' in Afshar, H (ed) *Women Development and Survival in the Third World*, London, Longmans.

Family Violence Prevention Fund (1997), News Flash, 24 November, www.fvfp.org.

Heise, L (1994) Violence Against Women: The Hidden Health Burden, Washington DC, World Bank Discussion Paper 255.

Howard, R (1986) 'An African Concept of Human Rights' in Vincent, R J (ed) *Foreign Policy and Human Rights*, Cambridge: Cambridge University Press, in association with The Royal Institute Of International Affairs.

Huq, N (5 August 1998), Naripokkho, personal correspondence.

Johnson, H (1996) *Dangerous Domains: Violence Against Women in Canada*, Scarborough Ontario, Canada, Nelson Canada.

Kabeer, N (1992), 'From Fertility Reduction to Reproductive Choice: Gender Perspectives on Family Planning', IDS Discussion Paper.

Kerr, J (ed) (1993) *Ours By Right: Womens Rights as Human Rights*, London, Zed.

Leng, C H (1988) 'Babies to Order: Recent Population Policies in Malaysia and Singapore' in Agarwal, B (ed) *Structures of Patriarchy*, London, Zed.

Mayer, E A (1995) 'Cultural Particularism as a Bar to Womens Rights: Reflections on Middle Eastern Experience' in Peters, J and Wolper, A (eds) *Womens Rights Human Rights: International Feminist Perspectives*, New York, Routledge.

Moser, C (1989) 'Gender Planning in the Third World: Meeting Practical and Strategic Gender Needs' in *World Development*, Vol 17, No 11, pp 1799–1825.

Naripokkho, Combatting Acid Violence in Bangladesh, Information leaflet , Dhaka Bangladesh (undated).

National Committee on Violence Against Women (1993) National Strategy on Violence Against Women, Canberra, Australian Government Publication Service.

Pearson, R (1993) 'Global Change and Insecurity: Are Women the Problem or the Solution?', in Baud, I and Smyth, I (eds.) *Searching for Security*, Routledge.

Peters, J and Wolper, A (eds) (1995) *Women's Rights Human Rights: International Feminist Perspectives*, New York, Routledge.

Robie, D (1997) Crime: PNG Women Declare War on Gang Rape, http://jsa-44.hum.uts.edu.au/acij/cafepacific/resources/aspac/rape.html.

Sen, P (1997) A Basket of Resources: Womens Resistance to Domestic Violence in Calcutta, PhD thesis, University of Bristol.

Sen, P (1998) 'Domestic Violence, Deportation and Women's Resistance: Notes on Managing Intersectionality', *Development in Practice*, Oxfam UK, November 1998.

Tanzanian Media Women's Association (1994) How Common is Sexual Assault in Tanzania? in Davies (ed) *Women and Violence: Realities and Responses worldwide*, pp76–84.

Thomas, D Q (1994) 'In Search of Solutions: Women's Police Stations in Brazil' in Davies, M (ed) *Women and Violence: Realities and Responses Worldwide*, London, Zed.

UNDP (1990–1997) Human Development Report, Oxford, Oxford University Press.

UNIFEM (1992) Fact Sheet on Gender Violence, A Statistics for Action Fact Sheet, New York, UNIFEM.

Wilson, M, Johnson, H and Daly, M (1995) 'Lethal and Non-Lethal Violence against Wives' in *Canadian Journal of Criminology*, July , pp 331–361.

Womankind Worldwide (1990) '"We Will Suffer no More": The Elimination of Violence Against Women', London: Womankind Worldwide.

World Bank, (1993) World Development Report, Oxford, Oxford University Press.

Zorza, J (1994) Woman Battering: High costs and the State of the Law, Clearing House Review 28.

Working towards a world free from violence against women: UNIFEM's contribution

Noeleen Heyzer

Since International Women's Year in 1975, violence against women has become a pressing concern for governments and the international community. This article discusses UNIFEM's multi-faceted approach to addressing violence against women at many levels. Key activities are resourcing projects and programmes, regional awareness-raising campaigns, and sharing learning on best practice.

The facts and the numbers are stunning: roughly 60 million women who should be alive today are 'missing' because of gender discrimination. In the United States, a woman is physically abused by her intimate partner every 9 seconds. Every day, another 6,000 girls are genitally mutilated. In India, more than 5,000 women are killed each year in the notorious 'dowry murders'. In the Rwanda nightmare more than 15,000 women were raped in one year.[1] Women in the North and the South live at risk of physical harm in ways which have no direct parallels for men. In every nation, violence or the threat of it, particularly at home, reduces the range of choices open to women and girls and narrows their options in almost every sphere of life, public and private — at home, in school, in the workplace, and in most community spaces. It limits women's choices directly by destroying their health, disrupting their lives, and constricting the scope of their activity; indirectly, it erodes their self-confidence and self-esteem. Ultimately, violence hinders women's full participation in society.

The difficult task of eradicating violence against women, a universal pandemic for millennia, cannot be underestimated. Research findings both in the North and the South have shown that violence against women occurs throughout their lives. It can extend from prebirth and infancy (for example, sex-selected abortion and infanticide) to old age (for example, violence against widows and elder abuse). Violence affects women of every nation, ideology, class, race, and ethnic group. It is exacerbated by poverty, but cannot be cured *exclusively* with economic remedies. In the short term, the overarching priority is to ensure that protection mechanisms are in place which ensure women's safety, and to respond appropriately to cases of abuse by bringing perpetrators to justice and offering medical and legal remedies to survivors. In the longer term, our challenge must be to reverse the rentrenched attitudes, gender stereotypes, and power structures which lie at the root of this pandemic.

With these precepts in mind, this article discusses UNIFEM's multi-faceted approach to addressing violence against women at many levels. The strategies we are using are changing continuously as we gain experience and learn new lessons about how we can fight violence against women more effectively.

Placing violence against women on the world agenda

UNIFEM's approach should first, however, be placed in the context of international efforts to eradicate violence against women since the International Women's Year in 1975. At the beginning of the United Nations World Decade for Women (1976–85), the issue of violence against women was not on the agenda, which called for equality, development, and peace. When the International Women's Year World Conference convened in Mexico City in 1975, the proceedings merely reflected a general awareness that domestic violence was problematic, and that women would benefit from more family counselling and more responsive family courts. Yet as the international women's movement has gained strength, public awareness of the dimensions and impact of the problem has grown at all levels of society.

Every country has acknowledged the existence of gender-based violence, and it is now agreed to be one of the major obstacles to all three of the goals of the Decade for Women. Discussions at world conferences on women in Copenhagen (1980) and Nairobi (1985) recognised domestic violence as an obstacle to equality, and an intolerable offence to human dignity. In 1985, the United Nations General Assembly passed its first resolution on violence against women, advocating concerted and multi-disciplinary action, within and outside the UN system, to combat domestic violence. However, it was the World Conference on Human Rights in Vienna in 1993 which really brought the issue of violence against women on to the international agenda. The global campaign for women's human rights, undertaken by a loose coalition of women's human rights advocates from around the world, succeeded in making governments acknowledge that violence against women is a fundamental violation of their human rights (Bunch and Reilly, 1994).

In 1993, the UN adopted the Declaration on the Elimination of Violence against Women, which defines the phenomenon and recommends measures to combat it. As Charlotte Bunch, Roxana Carrillo and Riman Shore have pointed out, this UN Declaration is a landmark document for three reasons.

• It situates violence against women squarely within the discourse on human rights. The declaration affirms that women are entitled to equal enjoyment and protection of all human rights and fundamental freedoms, including liberty and security of person, and to freedom from torture or other cruel, inhuman, or degrading treatment or punishment.

• It enlarges the concept of violence against women to reflect the real conditions of women's lives. The declaration recognises not only physical, sexual, and psychological violence, but also the threat of such harm; it addresses violence against women within the family setting, as well as within the general community; and it confronts the issue of violence perpetrated or condoned by the state.

• It points to the gender-based roots of violence. Gender violence is not random violence in which victims happen to be women and girls: rather, the 'risk factor' is being female (Bunch, Carrillo and Shore, 1998).

In 1979, the UN adopted the Convention on the Elimination of all Forms of Discrimination Against Women (CEDAW). This 'Bill of Rights' for women marked a significant milestone in articulating a framework of non-discrimination and equality for women. In requiring states to regulate private as well as public gender-based violence, CEDAW also elaborated on the meaning of discrimination to include issues related to violence against women. General Recommendation No. 19 of CEDAW notes:

'Traditional attitudes by which women are regarded as subordinate to men or as having stereotyped roles perpetuate widespread practices involving violence or coercion, such as family violence and abuse, forced marriage, dowry death, acid attacks, and female circumcision. Such prejudices and practices may justify gender-based violence as a form of protection or control of women. The effect of such violence on the physical and mental integrity of women is to deprive them of equal enjoyment, exercise, and knowledge of human rights and fundamental freedoms.'

Responses to the pandemic

At its 50th session on 4 March 1994, the Commission on Human Rights adopted a resolution that established the post of Special Rapporteur on Violence against Women. The Special Rapporteur on Violence has since worked to gather information on violence against women (and its causes and consequences) from governments, treaty bodies, specialised agencies, other special rapporteurs responsible for various human rights questions, and from inter-government and non-government organisations, including women's organisations. In UNIFEM's assessment, the Special Rapporteur's recommendations on necessary measures for preventing, combating, and eradicating violence against women at the national, regional, and international levels have been critical in sustaining the prominence of the issue in the international community. They have also guided governments and international actors toward effective courses of action.

The Fourth World Conference on Women held in 1995 in Beijing remains an important landmark in consolidating the gains made in the commitments to eradicating violence against women, and the analysis of gender-based violence as a human-rights issue. The Beijing Platform for Action (PFA, 1995) defines clear objectives and recommends strategies for the prevention and eradication of gender-based violence. It is certain to serve as an important standard for measuring progress achieved through concrete actions at all levels.

Following the Beijing Conference, the UN General Assembly mandated the Commission on the Status of Women to be responsible for a follow-up process to monitor the implementation of the PFA. Most recently, the CSW completed its review of the implementation of critical areas of concern in the Beijing PFA relating to violence and the human rights of women and girls. In its conclusions and recommendations, it particularly noted the UN General Assembly's creation of a Trust Fund in Support of Actions to Prevent and Eliminate Violence against Women at UNIFEM as a positive example. Over the past few years, UNIFEM has been at the forefront of work on violence against women within the UN system, supporting initiatives to combat violence against women in strong partnership with women's rights NGOs and governments engaged in this work, and taking significant steps to incorporate the issues into its own programmes. Apart from funding projects which combat violence against women, UNIFEM has also launched Regional Awareness Campaigns as a means of prevention.

1. The UNIFEM Trust Fund in Support of Actions to Eliminate Violence against Women

Created at UNIFEM under the guidance of a UN General Assembly resolution, the Trust Fund translates the recommendations adopted in Beijing into concrete action. The Trust Fund adheres to the definition of violence against women which is articulated in the Declaration on the Elimination of Violence against Women, as 'any act of gender-based violence that results in, or is likely to result in, physical, sexual or psychological harm or suffering to women, including threats of such acts, coercion or arbitrary deprivation of liberty, whether occurring in public or in private life'.

The Trust Fund aims to fund innovative and catalytic projects which are strategically placed to have a broad impact, and which contribute to learning about the most effective ways of eliminating violence against women. Projects focus on a wide range of innovative initiatives in the areas of education, capacity building, violence prevention and deterrence, awareness raising and the reversal of ingrained attitudes, and action-oriented research.

The Trust Fund began funding projects in 1997, and to date has supported 59 projects in 49 countries. Grants have been disbursed in Africa, Asia and the Pacific, Latin America and the Caribbean, Central and Eastern Europe, and the Commonwealth of Independent States.

Many of the projects that receive our funding focus on our first major theme, of human-rights abuse of women within the family. Working with youths, two projects in South Africa and Mexico aim to sensitise adolescents in high schools; in Surinam, another project works with young women involved in their first relationships with men. Through facilitated discussions and drama productions as well as through training peers to become counsellors and to form and lead support groups, the Surinam project aims to introduce alternative conflict-resolution methods and, most of all, to uproot damaging stereotypes and attitudes. In Pakistan, a project is working to introduce women's human rights into school curricula in primary as well as secondary schools.

Some projects encourage communities to take direct action against domestic violence. In the Philippines, a project trains men and women to improve awareness and responsiveness to domestic violence in remote communities. In Ethiopia, women community leaders are being trained as paralegals to provide legal counselling to women. A unique project in Trinidad and Tobago conducts workshops for men, women, and children over an entire weekend, using a variety of methods including interactive role-playing.

Highlighting the role of national and local governments in eradicating violence against women is key to some projects UNIFEM is assisting. In Peru, local government officials are trained to design and implement programmes in their provinces to respond to domestic violence. In Honduras, the Mayor of Comayagua has been enlisted to co-ordinate a project implemented by government and NGO partners in a neighbourhood with a particularly high incidence of gender-based violence.

The UNIFEM Trust Fund is also supporting work which aims to enable professionals to fulfil their roles and responsibilities in relation to women who face domestic violence. In India, judges are trained in legal remedies and law-enforcement methods which protect women. In Botswana, police staff are being trained to respond to battery and assault of women by their partners. In Colombia and Venezuela, health professionals are being taught to identify cases of violent abuse as well as reporting and counselling skills. A project in Kyrgyzstan trains journalists in Central Asia on gender-sensitive reporting.

Projects also include some which aim to reverse ingrained cultural attitudes to violence against women. Media campaigns, radio programmes, films, and videos, as well as symbolic "tribunals" featuring personal testimonies of women survivors of violence are being funded in various contexts, ranging from East Africa to Asia to Latin America and the Caribbean.

The second important theme in projects funded by the Trust Fund is war crimes against women. UNIFEM's Trust Fund supports projects in countries devastated by war and civil strife, where women struggle to recover from the physical, emotional, and economic violence to which they have been subjected. Projects range from trauma-management training in Algeria and Bosnia to encouraging public debate of the issues through popular plays in the local languages of Burundi and Congo.

Third, the Trust Fund focuses on violations of women's bodily integrity. These involve patterns of coercion and violence, and practices aimed at controlling women's sexuality and reproduction, which reach across wider social, cultural, and economic institutions. There are four major themes in this category: international economic and structural upheavals that result in the proliferation of new or revised forms of sexual and economic exploitation of women; violations of women's bodily integrity which are excused in the name of cultural or religious practice and expression; abuse as the result of forced conformity to heterosexual norms; and violation of the human rights of women who are physically challenged or disabled.

Today, the practice of FGM affects an estimated 85–114 million girls and women world-wide. FGM is practised in at least 26 African countries, in minority communities in some Asian countries, and by immigrant groups in Europe, Canada, Australia, and the United States. Female genital mutilation causes pain, trauma, and frequently severe physical complications, including bleeding, infection, infertility, and even death. It doubles the risk of maternal death during childbirth. Trust Fund projects focused on this area adopt a holistic approach to the issues, aiming to eradicate this harmful practice while remaining sensitive to the related complex social and economic issues. Thus, projects in Mali and Somalia work to sensitise women who perform excisions,[2] and train them in alternative income-generating activities, including midwifery. A project in Kenya involves local commu-

nities in developing alternative coming-of-age rituals which forego the harmful aspect of the traditional ritual.

A pilot project is focusing on crimes of 'femicide' in Palestinian society, where a man may kill an allegedly unfaithful, disobedient, or wilful wife, and be absolved on grounds of honour. The legal defence based on 'honour' and 'provocation by the victim' often requires little or no evidence, and results in unduly short prison terms for wife-murder, even when it is premeditated. The project is working to document cases, to recommend strategies for protecting potential victims, and to strengthen the legal system in order to deter perpetrators.

Projects which fall under the category of economic discrimination and exploitation are also supported by the Trust Fund. These respond to different forms of exploitation of women including sexual harassment and intimidation, in the workplace, in educational institutions, and elsewhere. The Trust Fund also seeks to support projects that address the problem of international trafficking in women, forced prostitution, and sexual slavery. The international sex trade affects the lives of millions of girls and their families. Young women are often enticed by offers of economic opportunity to leave their homes, only to find themselves sexual prisoners in foreign lands where they are often in flight from the law, ignorant of their rights and possible means of obtaining assistance. In some poor countries families are willing to sell female family members in circumstances of economic hardship. In Russia, a Trust Fund project seeks to raise awareness among high-risk groups, focusing specifically on orphaned girls and orphanage staff in remote provinces. In Nepal, a film is being produced which personalises the story of a young Nepalese girl who falls victim to the international sex trade.

Socio-economic violence in the workplace is experienced by many women. In the Philippines, the Trust Fund supports a project aimed at sensitising women migrant workers to the risks involved in employment abroad. The project informs them of their legal and human rights in such situations, as well as of means of improving their protection. Women who themselves have experienced violence as migrant workers will be trained to develop and produce a video documenting their own experiences, which will be used to warn and educate others. In Slovenia and Croatia, a project entitled 'How to Say No to the Boss' addresses the issue of sexual harassment in the workplace.

Finally, the Trust Fund supports projects aiming to eliminate political persecution of and discrimination against women enshrined in law. Gender-based civil and political violations of human rights experienced by women include gender-based persecution in detention, as well as state-mediated harassment and violation of basic political, civil, social, and economic rights. With growing numbers of women migrants and refugees globally, a system of human-rights protection based on membership of a nation-state is no longer adequate, especially where there is gender-blindness to the kinds of human rights violations that women in these situations face. In balancing the cultural and/or religious freedoms of groups against the rights of individuals, women's political and civil rights have all too often been sacrificed.

Trust Fund projects addressing this area have largely focused on building the capacity of women's groups to mobilise, network, and develop strategies for action. In Pakistan, a project is training Afghan women refugees in leadership skills. In Turkey, an experienced women's NGO will mobilise and train women's groups throughout the country to counter violence against women, including women from minority groups who suffer from state-sponsored infringement of their civil and political rights.

A Project Approval Committee for the Trust Fund is comprised of a wide range of UN organisations with expertise in various aspects of violence against women: UNDP (looking at gender-based violence as a development issue), UNICEF (concerned with protection of girls from violence), UNHCR (specifically concerned with violence against women refugees), UNFPA, UNAIDs and WHO (with an interest in the relationship between violence, sexual and reproductive health and rights, and public health in general) and the High Commissioner for Human Rights (championing a rights-based approach to combating violence against women; national machineries), as well as non-government agencies.

2. Regional awareness-raising campaigns on violence against women

The second component of UNIFEM's current work on violence against women is Regional Awareness Campaigns to prevent and eliminate violence against women. This component complements the Trust Fund, and it is intended that both initiatives should be mutually reinforcing. The Campaigns seek to introduce the issue of violence against women to the agendas of governments throughout the world, through raising awareness in the media, civil society, educational institutions, and the private sector as well as the public and government sectors. Each Regional Campaign highlights region-specific manifestations of violence against women and informs the public at large about the harmful consequencecs for women but also to society as a whole. Campaign activities ensure that continuing attention is drawn to existing commitments made by governments to ratify or to improve their compliance with CEDAW, and spell out the concrete steps which must still be taken at the national and regional levels.

The Campaigns involve UN agencies, civil society partners, and governments, to ensure that they are far-reaching and inclusive. The fact that the awareness-raising Campaigns are being supported by all agencies throughout the UN system considerably increases the chance that they will reap concrete results, by tying commitments by governments in the area of violence against women into the country-assistance agreements with the UN.

In Latin America and the Caribbean, the regional campaign is well underway: its slogan is 'A Life Free from Violence: It's Our Right'. In all countries of the region, highly publicised events have been organised around the 50th anniversary of the Universal Declaration of Human Rights. Campaign activities have been shaped as a celebration of achievements towards preventing and eliminating violence against women, realised through the work of activist groups and the commitment of national governments and regional organisations. At the same time, activities focus on the actions that must yet be taken towards achieving progress in the areas of legislative reform, improvement of enforcement mechanisms, and public education.

The Inter-Agency Campaign has launched an all-out awareness-raising strategy, which has involved extensive use of public fora to engage society in a public dialogue and debate on ending violence against women. The Campaign will also address the human, social, and economic costs of violence against women and emphasise the need to empower women as valuable partners inside and outside the home. Powerful messages on ending violence against women will be highly visible through campaign posters, recognisable slogans against gender-based violence, radio spots on over 1,000 radio stations (in local languages), prominent personalities endorsing the campaign, information flyers distributed in popular magazines, press conferences, photography contests, and television spots.

A particularly vital campaign initiative is the involvement of local government and communities. The Municipality of Mexico City, for instance, will co-ordinate a challenge to municipalities throughout the region to present examples of the ways in which they are promoting and protecting women's human rights. Three examples will be selected for wide dissemination and learning. A follow-up to this process will be the establishment of an exchange and co-operation programme among Latin American municipalities to enhance the enjoyment of women's rights. It is hoped that the range of Campaign strategies will lead to mass public awareness about the issues, and foster the political will of policy and decision-makers and legislators to revise national legislation in order to make it increasingly responsive to the issues of gender-based violence. In 19 countries in the region, thus far, governments have agreed to do precisely this.

Africa's Regional Campaign also involves national governments, women's groups, UN agencies, and the media, to promote the message of a life free from violence and poverty for women and girls. It is planned that the Africa Campaign will highlight gender-based violence in war situations. Violence against women is often used as a systematic weapon of destruction; in a post-conflict context, widowed women become heads of household, yet often remain disenfranchised of their legal and human rights. Additionally, the Campaign will make visible the factors that contribute to violence against women at all levels of society and the changes necessary to eradicate violence against women. These include facing the challenge of meeting economic burdens; recognising the integral links between promoting Africa's economic development and the need to safeguard women's human rights; complying with the international norms and standards which bind African governments to promote, protect, and respect the human rights of women; and bringing about changes in laws, policies, and attitudes to eliminate violence against women and girls. The Campaign will use similar strategies to those used successfully in the Latin American and Caribbean Campaign, and emphasise the linkages between violence and women's continued marginalisation from economic, political and social decision making processes. Other campaigns are soon to follow in Asia and the Pacific region, Central and Eastern Europe, and the Commonwealth of Independent States.

3. *Sharing learning*

We are developing a 'Learning Component' for the Trust Fund, which will analyse the results of Trust Fund initiatives, and suggest ways of shaping more effective strategies for combating violence against women.

In conjunction with developing the Trust Fund's learning component, we are also committed to documenting and sharing success stories, innovative strategies, and challenges in preventing and eliminating violence against women. We will develop a comprehensive UN information base with details of best practices and proven strategies for preventing and eliminating violence against women. The hope is to stimulate replication of, and innovation in developing, effective models for combating gender-based violence and to foster partnerships between government, the UN system, civil society, and the private sector.

UNIFEM will hold a global teleconference to highlight innovative actions which are emerging from Regional Awareness-raising Campaigns undertaken during 1998, as well as examples of the most innovative initiatives supported by the Trust Fund. The teleconference, which will take place on 24 November — on the eve of the internationally celebrated '16 Days of Activism against Violence against Women' — seeks to bring visibility to the work of civil society, governments, and UN agencies in addressing violence against women.

Towards the future

Strengthening enforcement mechanisms in response to violence against women

Although the work of the Regional Campaigns and the Trust Fund concen-trates on the issue of violence against women, the deep-seated connection between violence against women and women's human rights calls for complementary work aimed at promoting the realisation of those rights. At the moment, in the wake of the Beijing Conference and the almost simultaneous exposure of the atrocities against women in Rwanda and the former Yugoslavia, it seems more possible than ever to mobilise effectively against systemic oppression of women. Women have an enormous stake in building societies at peace. The sharing mutual care and co-operation which underpin happy, stable communities cannot flourish without peace; these values must be at the centre of our development strategies. The dismantling of power structures in which violence is used and tolerated as a tool in the oppression and degradation of women will take energy, determination, and creative strategies.

UNIFEM recently supported the participation of women's human-rights advocates in the Diplomatic Conference to establish an International Criminal Court in Rome during June/July 1998. These advocates participated in order to ensure that the establishment of a permanent criminal court would have the best possible potential impact for women all over the world. The ICC must be an effective independent body, with the capacity to address all aspects of the crimes within its jurisdiction, including aspects of gender. The standards established at this Conference could have far-reaching implications, setting standards for national courts and legal systems in general. They could serve as the basis or a model for new laws or legal reforms which women are lobbying for at the national level, particularly laws dealing with violence-related and other gender-based crimes.

Strengthening capacity to use international legal instruments

UNIFEM is currently developing innovative approaches in order to link the human-rights norms and standards established by UN Conventions and Treaty Bodies with national-level efforts to advocate for women's human rights. In its aim to move CEDAW, a pivotal international treaty, from vision to reality, UNIFEM has developed an array of initiatives to encourage universal ratification, to strengthen the awareness and capacity of women's organisations for the use of the Convention in their advocacy work, and to collaborate with other partners in the UN system to support the work of the CEDAW Committee and the strengthening of the Convention itself. An example of these efforts is the global training programme on CEDAW, originally co-sponsored by UNIFEM and International Women's Rights Action Watch Asia-Pacific. For the past two years, this programme has invited civil society advocates of women's human rights from countries which report to CEDAW to a global training session in New York.

To date, this global initiative has trained a resource pool of 33 women from 17 countries which report to the CEDAW Committee. These training sessions aim to strengthen the understanding of women's rights advocates of the Convention and the Committee's working methods, and how these apply to their advocacy work at the national level. They are also often called on to act as a resource to the Committee and to their governments. UNIFEM is committed to replicating such training at the national and regional levels, and to continuing to facilitate the connection between global and local advocacy based on the principles of the Women's Convention.

Facilitating Information Exchange

Fostering effective access to and exchange of information about effective strategies is critical to the process of eliminating violence against women. UNIFEM has recently supported two initiatives which strive to create widely accessible means to promote, facilitate, and shape broad-based, continuous

advocacy strategies for women's human rights, and which aim to combat the abuse of women's human rights by strengthening advocates' capacity to engage in informed and sustained advocacy at the local, national, regional, and international levels.

The first strategy is the initiative of the Sisterhood is Global Institute in New York to create a leadership and human-rights programme, to help women define and secure their human rights in Muslim societies. This innovative programme has designed a 'leadership-building project' which aims to enhance women's leadership capabilities at various levels of communal and inter-community involvement. This is combined with a technology-based initiative, fostering links between the project and other similar activities throughout the Muslim world. Through a series of training sessions and workshops on women's human rights and the use of computers and the Internet for research and advocacy, the programme will enhance women's leadership capabilities and increase awareness of women's human rights at the national level in nine countries. It will also enhance women's ability to participate in defining their rights, establish communication nodes throughout the Muslim world in order to gather and exchange information related to issues of women's human rights, and facilitate a dialogue between women activists from the Muslim world.

The second such project is the creation of a women's human rights joint information and communication technology project on the Internet. This project attempts to address several problems which limit the effectiveness of women's human rights advocates. These include the lack of readily accessible information at national level; the need for a venue where advocates can come together to exchange information about their separate advocacy efforts, or to plan collective advocacy strategies; and the need for critical training and resources relating to leadership development, institution building, UN advocacy, human-rights fact-finding, reporting, and fund-raising, and using information and communication technology.

This initiative will develop a jointly sponsored information system on the world-wide web — accessible through the Internet — on women's human rights. The system will provide access to crucial information (such as current global campaigns; news and action alerts; UN events and meetings; resources for capacity building; links to partners; and a calendar of government, UN, and NGO women's human-rights events) as well as an on-line space to exchange experiences and best practices at the national, regional, and international levels. Discussion groups, conferences, and other networking activities will be facilitated, and up-to-date information on contemporary women's human rights issues will be widely available in a clear and accessible format.

The demand is enormous — women's groups and, increasingly, governments, are working toward a world free from violence, where women's lives are free from fear and brutalisation. 1998 is the 50th Anniversary of the Universal Declaration of Human Rights. We must seize this commemorative year as a challenge to recharge our spirits, to fight for change, and to reassert our deep commitment to UNIFEM's core belief that women's rights are human rights. UNIFEM is committed to expending all our efforts to help forge the political will to implement the programmes and policies necessary to enable every woman in the world to feel the power and freedom of knowing that she is able to live a life free from violence, and to exercise all of her human rights. In this year of anniversaries and reviews pivotal to the United Nations' principles of human rights, we know that there can be no sustainable communities or development without the attainment of peace and women's human rights.

Noeleen Heyzer is the Executive Director of the United Nations Development Fund for Women (UNIFEM). In this role, she continues to shape UNIFEM's role as provider of strategic and technical know-how to the UN system in the area of women's empowerment and gender equality. A native of Singapore, Noeleen Heyzer holds a Ph.D. in Social Sciences from the University of Cambridge, UK.

For additional information about UNIFEM, please contact: UNIFEM, 304 East 45th Street, 6th Floor, New York, NY 10017, E-mail: unifem@undp.org; fax: (212) 906-6705; http://www.unifem.undp.org

Notes

1 Statistics quoted in this article are taken from the UN *Human Development Report*, UNDP, 1995, and 'The Intolerable Status Quo: Violence Against Women and Girls', by Charlotte Bunch, in *The Progress of Nations*, UNICEF, 1997.
2 The most serious form of FGM.

References

Bunch C, 'The Intolerable Status Quo: violence against women and girls', in *The Progress of Nations*, UNICEF, 1997.

Bunch C and Reilly N, *Demanding Accountability: The Global Campaign and Vienna Tribunal for Women*, UNIFEM/Centre for Global Leadership, New York, 1994.

Bunch C, Carrillo R and Shore R, 'Violence against women' — background paper for 1995 UNDP Human Development Report, in Stromquist N (ed.), *Women in the Third World*, Garland Publishing, New York, 1998.

Human Development Report UNDP, New York, 1995.

Forced marriage, forced sex:

the perils of childhood for girls

Mariam Ouattara, Purna Sen, and Marilyn Thomson

A new inter-agency group, the Forum on the Rights of Girls and Women in Marriage, has been formed to investigate how early marriage, non-consensual marriage, and rape within marriage affect girls and women. Comparing case studies from Nepal, West Africa, and India, the authors argue that, to be effective, we must address cultural practices harming girls separately.

Anti-Slavery International, CHANGE, the Child Rights Information Network (CRIN), International Planned Parenthood Federation (IPPF), and Save the Children Fund (UK) have recently come together in a Forum on the Rights of Girls and Women in Marriage. The aim of this inter-agency Forum is to gather information and reach a better understanding of the scale of these issues, and of the legal, social, and health implications of early and non-consensual marriage and of rape within marriage. In coming together we are looking to discuss common concerns in relation to these issues, to share experiences, and to identify common agendas for advocacy and policy development on the question of human rights within marriage for women and girls — involving changes in the education of boys, too.

Three bodies of work, from three of the organisations involved in the Forum, form the basis of this article: research into child marriage in parts of West Africa by Anti-Slavery International; an investigation of children's views of early marriage by Save the Children; and research into women's resistance to domestic violence in Calcutta[2]

which is the basis of a new campaign by CHANGE. The conclusion points to the need to investigate and advocate for legislative and policy approaches to tackle non-consensual marriage and sex, as well as servile or slave-like conditions of marriage, and to generate and disseminate successful approaches.

Force and human rights

The forcing of one human being by another is an infringement of many human rights that are promised to all, but are systematically denied to girls across many countries (see for example Ashworth 1986, Bunch 1997). Adult women experience some such infringements, which include being forced into marriage and into sex within marriage, without the opportunity of giving consent. These wrongs can be similar for both girls and women, but this article draws specific attention to girls and young women, focusing on both forced and early marriage, and on the nature of sexual force within marriage.

The denial of the rights of girls continues on a widespread scale and often centres on marriage; that is, the most private sphere. Despite the potential of various international conventions and conferences — such as the full body of human rights instruments, including the 1979 Convention on the Elimination of All Forms of Discrimination Against Women (CEDAW), the 1989 Convention on the Rights of the Child (CRC), and the 1995 Beijing Platform for Action — the lives of many girls remain unchanged. The consequences for girls are grave and pervasive, in terms of health, social status, and the incapacity to determine their own lives. Not only does this mean that much more work needs to be done around implementation of international legal instruments, but it also highlights, as argued in this article, the need for greater recognition of the more difficult aspects of the perils of girlhood, such as marital rape of child brides.

Child marriage, forced marriage

In their work, both SCF and Anti-Slavery International prioritise the need to highlight and work against the practice of child marriage. This section draws on Anti-Slavery International's experience in three African countries, and on SCF's experience in Nepal.

Countries throughout the world, including many African countries, have ratified most international conventions and regional standards on human rights and made great efforts to integrate them into their national legislation. Yet, in many of these countries, attitudes and customs seen as 'traditional' continue to subordinate women and girls. These include human-rights violations such as female genital mutilation, domestic violence, deprivation of land and property, and child and forced marriage. In deprived rural areas in most West African countries, many ten or 11 year-old girls look forward to a bleak future: to work as a domestic servant, as a commercial sex worker, or to be given away as a child bride.

In Cotonou and Porto-Novo in Southern Benin, early marriage is a common practice. Girls as young as ten to 13 are kidnapped from their families and taken to their husband. Girls are betrothed at or before birth by their parents, in respect of friendship or based on a system of exchanging women between ethnic groups within the community. The husband-to-be and his family may have given presents (*dadaho*) or provided services (*glodian*) to their future in-laws according to custom. Parents feel a strong obligation to respect the pledge, forcing the girl to marry the man they have chosen for her. It is not unknown for desperate girls, unwilling to marry a man they do not know or love, to commit suicide.

In Burkina Faso, the practice of child marriage is widespread. Around the capital, Ouagadougou, three Catholic religious centres shelter girls who have run away from early and forced marriage. Many of these girls escape in dangerous conditions, walking from rural areas for three to seven days to the centres. They hide in trees during the day and walk at night-time. Both economically and psychologically, they are in a grave situation. Their families usually disown them, so that they are without moral or financial support; and the religious sisters commonly pressure them to join the orders in which they find refuge. Puksata, a local NGO in Burkina Faso, is working with the religious centres to provide vocational training to the girls and mediating between the families and their daughters.

In Côte d'Ivoire, the Association Beninoise des Femmes Juristes (ABFJ) and the Association Ivoirienne de Defense des Droits des Femmes (AIDDF) are active in campaigning and lobbying on the issue of child marriage. Fanta Keita, aged 15, was jailed two years ago for the murder of her husband. Fanta Keita had been betrothed to her cousin as a small girl; at the age of 15, she was taken to the capital to join the husband whom she had never met. She escaped and returned home, but was beaten and sent back. She fled a second time, but again was returned to the man her parents had chosen for her. With no way out, Fanta took desperate action and stabbed her husband, killing him. In Côte d'Ivoire and Benin, ABFJ and AIDDF have developed a training programme in the provinces where child marriage is predominant, to educate the public on the rights of women and girls, and to furnish the national legislation with information to improve or abolish some of the customs associated with early marriage.

Early marriage is also an issue in Nepal: according to the 1992 Children's Act, early marriage is defined as marriage under 16 years for girls and 18 for boys. SCF has been running a health project in the Bhutanese refugee camps since 1992,[3] and this has included a Children's Programme since 1997. Here, the practice of child marriage is common for boys and girls under 18 years of age (90 per cent were girls between 12–17 years old). SCF has undertaken a child-centred participatory research project (Umesh Kumar Kattel 1997) to identify the reasons and the effects on children's health, education and family life. A range of participatory research tools were used with children, parents, health workers, and staff in the refugee camps.

The SCF study found that the majority of these marriages were arranged by parents, grandparents, and guardians, and identified a range of reasons: the girls were required to provide domestic help for the boy's family; grandparents wanted to see their granddaughter settled before they died; parents believed that marriage of girls before menstruation is 'holiness', or wished to remove children from a situation where there was domestic violence between parents. In some cases, the children were forced into marriage because of pregnancy; in others, the parents' feared inter-caste relationships or that their children would elope with someone who was unsuitable.

Some children had chosen a love marriage at an early age, for different reasons. These included having nowhere to go and a lack of recreational activities in the camps; lack of guidance by parents; the frustrations of staying in the camps for a long time; and a desire to find security because life as a refugee meant an uncertain future and a disorganised social environment. Girls' expectations included a belief that they would have a better life after marriage in terms of better clothes, food, and facilities, and revealed a desire to get away from a home life where girls were being abused by step-parents or guardians as well as a lack of knowledge about the health and other consequences of early marriage. 'My step-mother forced me to marry. She said that if you do not marry the boy I find, you will be in trouble [...] Now for six months my husband has not talked to me or seen me, he is always angry with me', said one girl.

Among the many serious consequences of early marriage, for girls in particular, SCF's research identified health risks associated with pregnancy, child-bearing, and lack of care for the girls themselves when they were ill or in need. There were a high number of teenage pregnancies, many of which were identified as high-risk deliveries. A large number of the babies delivered to teenage mothers had a low birth weight (under 2.5 kilos) and the babies were at risk of contracting serious communicable diseases. Teenage mothers lacked knowledge about caring for and breast-feeding their babies. The neo-natal and peri-natal mortality rate was high, as was the still-birth rate. Girls themselves suffered a lack of nutritious food, love, care, and support while sick, pregnant and/or breast-feeding — leading to anaemia and malnutrition. The burden of housework left little time for rest and leisure.

Social consequences included a detrimental effect on the education of both sexes. The majority of boys and girls interviewed had dropped out of school after early marriage (only one respondent — a boy — had started again), which seriously hampered their educational and social development. 'My wife and I could have been studying in higher classes as friends if my father and relatives had not forced us for marriage when I was 14 years and my wife was 12 years old', said one boy. The general perception of the community involved in the research was that children were not allowed to continue at school once they were married. In fact, the camp schools did not have a clear policy on this; they stipulated that children could only continue if they married with their parents' consent, and had their written permission to continue at school. If these conditions were met, husband and wife could not attend the same school, as this might cause problems in the classrooms and encourage other children to get married.

SCF's research indicated that, once married, the children faced problems in their family and social relationships. They were overloaded with domestic and family responsibilities and had no spare time to see their friends and family or to participate in social activities. The girls were often badly treated by their husbands' families: they were overburdened with domestic chores, shouted at, and mentally abused. For boys, life was easier; but they now faced conflicting situations in their families because their parents and elders did not give them the love and attention they received previously. They were now considered mature and were expected to take care of their wives and to please their parents and leaders.

The study concluded that early marriage has serious health and social implications for children, and made a number of proposals for action and further study. These include raising awareness among children and parents through informal educational approaches; designing sex education and marriage guidance programmes to be introduced through the school curriculum; revising the schools' policies about married children's access; creating opportunities for informal and vocational training;

and involving married children in a youth-education programme on the consequences and negative effects of early marriage.

Rape and sexual abuse in marriage[4]

Child marriage must be understood as a situation of danger for girls, characterised by widespread rape and a life of servility. CHANGE is beginning a major programme on non-consensual sex within marriage which will include the experience of girl-wives. Part of the programme is a world-wide survey on whether or not governments have adopted legal and policy initiatives to tackle these practices, wherever they are found. The survey will also identify the strategies which brought about positive changes, the circumstances in which they were won, and how they are being implemented. For states where no such initiatives exist, CHANGE will explore the obstacles in the path of progress. Outcomes of the survey will be used to lobby for change, at the international and national levels, and successful strategies will be published and disseminated widely. The following discussion of issues facing young girls who undergo early marriage in India draws on a study in Calcutta undertaken by Purna Sen (1997).

In recent years, public knowledge of, recognition of, and action against certain forms of domestic violence against women have increased in many countries — but much of this has focused on physical abuse alone. Sexual abuse remains less well recognised but can have devastating consequences, denying women's bodily integrity and control, causing untold numbers of unwanted pregnancies, and a range of negative health implications, not least of all the risk of HIV infection.

The absence of discussion about sexual abuse has serious consequences. First, the opportunities for young women suffering such abuse to speak about their experiences are negligible, so they cannot easily seek help.

Second, governments and their agencies participate in maintaining this silence, through inaction on sexual abuse and marital rape of women in principle, and of young girls in practice. This precludes both punishment of rapists and protection of victims, and amounts to state collusion with rapists. Third, research (Sen 1997) suggests that sexual violence in marriage is associated with a greater likelihood of separation than physical violence alone. While this is a just outcome in freeing women and young girls from abuse, in many societies their communities are at best uncomfortable in handling single female adulthood. Women who leave their marriage face an immense range of problems, from social ostracism through to violent attacks, including rape, and economic destitution.

While all of the above applies both to child and adult wives, the particular circumstances of young girls should cause great concern. Sen's research in Calcutta found that, compared to women who married after the age of 15, girls who marry young are more likely to be illiterate and to have no experience of formal education. Other aspects in which the younger brides differ from older women include a greater likelihood of sterilisation and dowry payments. Younger brides are also less likely to come into contact with government or voluntary organisations, to have bank accounts in their own names, or to own assets — although they are more likely to carry debt-servicing commitments, despite having lower employment rates. Sadly, young brides also report a higher incidencece of infant mortality, with over one-third saying that at least one child had died after birth.

The continuing practice of child marriage contributes to a widespread experience of sexual abuse: it is, in effect, the socially legitimised institutionalisation of marital rape — the rape of (sometimes very) young girls. In Sen's research, almost half of the women in the sample had been married at or below the age of 15, and the youngest was merely seven years old. This age group

(15 and below) had one of the highest rates of vulnerability to sexual violence in marriage, second only to those where dowry had been paid. Women spoke of sexual intercourse before the onset of menstruation, early and very painful sex, and many still continued to be forced into sexual activity by their husbands. Many of these cases meet the narrow definition of marital rape in Indian law. In almost half the cases of forced sex or marital rape, the girl-wives had made their husbands aware of their unwillingness to have sex or of pain during sex, but in 80 per cent of these cases the rapes continued.

The marriage of young girls is often made more traumatic by the absence of public or familial discussion of sexuality and puberty. Girls' access to information on sexuality in India is highly restricted, if there is any at all, and they typically begin marital sexual relations in ignorance of what sex involves. Physical controls on girls' behaviour (particularly in urban areas) leaves them little room to mix with boys or to gain any sexual experience before marriage. Boys enjoy much greater freedoms and a wider range of discussion with their peers, which may include sexual talk. Many women in Sen's study spoke of the intense pain and fear of early sex. However, the absence of a vocabulary to discuss sexual violence denies girls access to support and increases their propensity to separate from husband-rapists.

Contrary to the common perception, and less common practice, of sexual abstinence until girls begin to menstruate, women reported that their husbands had forced sex upon them — raped them — before their periods had started. Others had slept in separate rooms from their husbands until they started to menstruate, but marital sex began almost immediately afterwards. Gita was married at the age of 14 to a man who had previously been married. When asked her why she had been married at such an early age, she said: 'One day when I was out tending to the goats, one got injured. I carried it back to the village and some of the blood was on my clothes. They all thought that I had started my periods and I got married three months later.'

Asked about sexual relations after marriage, she responded: 'It was very bad, very difficult. I had a lot of pain... I used to be scared when he came to get me and carry me to his bed. I used to cry and go to lie somewhere else, but he'd come and get me... When I came to visit my family, I didn't want to go back... My periods started two years after I got married. I told my [sister-in-law], and she thought I had started before I got married. Then they didn't let me cook or touch anything for three days. I only told you because you asked. I have never told anyone before.' Gita was 38 years old when she talked about these experiences; she had carried the pain and memory of sexual trauma alone for 24 years. It is hard to imagine the fear of sex and the shock it caused when she was first married.

The notion that the attainment of puberty should give free licence for sex to start are highly problematic, as Gita's example shows. The absence of discussion of sexual matters means that there is considerable room for confusion and mistakes. In effect, society tacitly permits sexual activity between men and very young girls; there is no possibility for girls to give or withhold personal permission for sexual activity. Equating a girl's attainment of puberty with a husband's licence to seek and force sex upon her denies each girl control over her own body, including her control over whether, when, and with whom she has sexual relations. The implications of this are vast. They include all the dangers associated with teenage motherhood which cause such uproar in the West — a disrupted education, the troubled parenting of babies by children, and negative implications for the girls' health, including the risks of childbirth.

The vast majority of countries have not criminalised rape in marriage; but sex with girls below a certain age (which varies) is usually covered by the standard rape legislation. Indian law recognises marital rape in cases where the girl is aged under 15 (Section 375, Indian Penal Code 1860, Act No 45 of 1860). However, this is mitigated by the religiously defined personal laws (see Socio-Legal Aid Research & Training Centre 1995:6, 24, 40): even the rape of a young girl between the ages of 12 and 15 years carries a lesser sentence if the rapist is married to the victim (Sarkar 1994:83). For adult wives, the only legal protection from husband-rapists exists if the couple have separated. It seems that, in the vast majority of cases, both the state and women's local communities are unwilling to confront the rape of young girls which goes on everyday, in the name of marriage. Young girls are raped; their abusers have the social legitimacy of marriage in which to carry out their assaults.

Conclusions

Far from being a time of innocence, pleasure, and freedom, childhood for girls in many countries is fraught with danger and potential pain. Forced marriage and forced sex within marriage are horrors that befall countless numbers of girls across the world. The vulnerabilities of young girls are shared with those of adult women. But girls experience them in a particular way because they are children and lack information about what are generally seen as, and should remain, adult issues of marriage and sex. The use of force in these situations is an infringement of girls' human rights.

If women's rights are to be effective, an assessment of existing traditional laws, and of who creates them and who implements them, should be carried out. This should involve women and girls who are affected by these laws. These assessments should screen the negative and positive effects of customs and practices, and facilitate a process of radical change, which will result in abandoning outdated laws and adopting practices which fit in with modern society. *Ad hoc* interventions are useful for urgent action, but we need long-term solutions, by working continuously on laws and implementation.

Although a number of international legal instruments such as CEDAW and the CRC provide a framework for promoting women's and girls' rights, the present situation, 'post Beijing', is disappointing. Before the World Conference in 1995, African groups met (in Dakar and Addis-Ababa) to consolidate their position: they emphasised that the problems of the girl child should not be subsumed under the heading of women, but should be maintained separately. This position was supported by the Save the Children Alliance and Anti-Slavery International, and was adopted by governments who attended the World Conference in the Platform for Action. However, three years on, violations of the rights of the child and abuse of the girl-child may well be increasing. The absence of proper legal and policy action frameworks to deal with women's and girls' rights, coupled with the lack of sanctions against these abuses, amount to state complicity and neglect of duty under international law to these citizens.

Our three organisations will be working together in the future on research, identifying common strategies, and advocacy to address these public-policy and human-rights issues through the Forum on the Rights of Women and Girls in Marriage. We invite researchers and organisations with an interest in these issues to join us in the Forum.

Mariam Ouattara is Programme Officer/Africa at Anti-Slavery International. Contact details: ASI, The Stableyard, Broomgrove Rd, London SW9 9TL, UK, Tel:+44 (171) 924 9555, Fax: +44 (171) 738 4110, E-mail:antislavery@gn.apc.org For Purna Sen's details see page 15. She can be contacted at Change, 106 Hatton Sq, London EC1N 7RJ, UK, Fax: +44 (171) 430 0254, E-mail: change_cic@compuserve.com
Marilyn Thomson is gender advisor for Save the Children Fund UK. Contact details: SCF (UK), Mary Datchelor House, 17 Grove Lane, Camberwell, London SE5 8RD, Fax: +44 (171) 703 5400, E-mail: m.thomson@scfuk.org.uk

Notes

1 The authors would like to thank Georgina Ashworth and Sarah Robinson for co-ordinating the writing of this article, and for their editorial input.
2 Funded by Bristol University Scholarship and the Tweedie Exploration Fellowship.
3 There are more than 97,000 refugees (almost half of them children) from Bhutan living in camps in Nepal. They started arriving in 1991, as a result of repression by Bhutanese government forces of the minority population of Nepalese ethnicity and Hindu religion.
4 This section draws on research conducted by Purna Sen (now of CHANGE), in Calcutta, India.

References

Ashworth, G, 1986, Of Violence and Violation: women and human rights, CHANGE.

Bunch, C, 1997, 'The Intolerable Status Quo: Violence Against Women and Girls' in *Progress of Nations*, UNICEF.

Sen, P, 1997, A Basket of Resources: Women's Resistance to Domestic Violence in Calcutta, PhD Thesis, University of Bristol.

Indian Penal Code 1860 (Act No 45 of 1860), Government of India, New Delhi, Orient Law House

Socio-legal Aid Research and Training Centre (SLARTC), 1995, Rights of Women in India, Calcutta, SLARTC.

Sarkar, L, 1994, 'Rape: A Human Rights versus a Patriarchal Interpretation' in *Indian Journal of Gender Studies*, Vol 1, No 1, January-June, pp 69-91.

Umesh Kuma Kattel, 'Study on the reasons and effects of child marriage in the Bhutanese refugee camps, Jhapa, Nepal' (internal document), SCF (UK), 1997.

The tears have not stopped, the violence has not ended:

Political upheaval, ethnicity, and violence against women in Indonesia

Galuh Wandita

In May of this year, student protests sparked off riots, looting, and arson all over Indonesia. After the political situation had stabilised, accounts emerged of women from ethnic minorities being targets of horrific violence. The subsequent publicity and debate have enabled women survivors to make their voices heard for the first time, and to take action together.

'Eyes are for seeing what is good and what is bad. Today we are gathered to share what we have witnessed, to share our experiences in order to work together. Together, we will stand tall.'
Statement of an East Timorese woman at a workshop with women survivors of violence, Dili, 8 August 1998.

Feminist research has, for decades, highlighted the way in which rape has been used as a tool for conquest in conflict throughout history and across the world (Brownmiller 1975). As women are viewed as objects in the general society in times of peace, this point of view will be reflected and heightened at a time of social strife. Women are seen as property of the enemy — thus justifying acts of plunder, forced possession, and destruction. Existing notions of masculinity, which equate it with the capacity to conquer and destroy, worsen in times of conflict.

The extent to which violence against women occur in Indonesia, both in peacetime and in the recent political unrest, is currently becoming clear. There is growing evidence that the Orde Baru (New Order) regime, under the iron hold of General Suharto for the past 32 years, has left a legacy of torture and sexual violence in its wake. The rape of Chinese-Indonesian women in Indonesia's capital, Jakarta, during riots in May 1998 has forced open a floodgate to testimonies of rape and sexual violence throughout the archipelago. In this short article, drawing on first-hand information and the ongoing research of a group of women activists of which I am a member, I aim to share some testimonies of women victims of violence, in order to further publicise the issues, and to reflect on how and why some of these stories have emerged, while others remain hidden.

The May 1998 riots

On 12 May 1998, the Indonesian public was shocked to hear of the cold-blooded murder of five university students at Trisakti University by the military, after months of student demonstrations all over Indonesia. News of the killings travelled swiftly; an outpouring of grief and anger was expressed in the morning press. Newspapers received faxes from members of the public condemning the act, including statements from women who identified themselves as usually apolitical housewives. On 21 May, General Suharto resigned from the presidency. Immediately after the killings of the students, on the evening of 12 May, Jakarta was besieged by riots. At the end of two days of rioting, 4,000 shops, 38 malls, and thousands of vehicles and homes were burned to the ground, leaving 1,198 dead — 27 from gunshot wounds. The worst looting and burning occured in commercial areas populated by Chinese-Indonesian merchants and their families, although it is important to note that casualties came from various ethnic groups. Most of those who perished in the fires which ravaged markets and shopping centres were people living in poverty.

The extent of the damage from the riots was documented by Volunteers for Humanity, a coalition of NGOs which had been established after attacks on the opposition Indonesian Democratic Party (PDI) by government-backed vigilante groups in July 1996.[1] During the May 1998 riots, Volunteers for Humanity opened aid centres throughout the city to provide emergency help to those in distress.

Almost two weeks after the mid-May riots, we began to receive reports on women of Chinese descent being raped. These reports initially came from church and Buddhist monastery-based groups, who requested assistance in supporting rape survivors but did not wish the issue to be publicised through the media.

This reluctance reflected this minority group's fear of further persecution. Approximately 8 million Indonesians (out of a population of 210 million) are categorised as 'naturalised' Indonesian citizens of Chinese descent. (This categorisation is ironic, given the fact that the pre-historic origins of the so-called 'indigenous' Indonesian population have been traced back to Yunnan.) During the independence movement, and in the early years of an independent Indonesia, Chinese-Indonesians took part in the struggle along with other ethnic groups which make up this nation of plural ethnic identities. However, the New Order regime banned the use of the Chinese language, later prohibited public Chinese celebrations, and ordered the use of Indonesian-style names. Modern tensions between different ethnic groups can be traced to colonial history, which divided the population into a hierarchy, with Europeans at the top, Indians, Arabs, and Chinese in the middle, and indigenous Indonesians at the bottom. Despite his anti-Chinese policies, Suharto granted privileges to a small group of Chinese-Indonesians, who quickly amassed vast wealth to support the regime.

First efforts to counter the violence

'After the two women were able to flee from those bastards, I approached them and embraced them. They asked me to find a safe way home. Because I am from the area, I know the short cuts. At the intersection to Cengkareng, I saw naked corpses of women — their faces covered with newspaper. They may have been raped. I saw dried blood, flies, around their private areas. When I returned from taking the two women home, I no longer saw those corpses. Who took them?'[2]

For Volunteers for Humanity, a dilemma emerged in relation to the religious groups' initial request for secrecy. We were torn between the urge to campaign publicly against these acts, and the desire to respect the request to keep them secret and thus protect survivors from the effects of publicity. Eventually, the story got out from other sources; we were immediately inundated by requests for confirmation by the press, demanding that organisations like ours should provide living proof that the rapes had actually occurred, in the form of a survivor willing to speak openly to the press. A lot of energy was spent explaining to the media that although we could provide information on the rapes and, particularly, on the pattern of violence which we were documenting, we could not divulge names because this would constitute a breach of privacy. In addition, the press wanted numbers, which we could not provide at the time because of the difficulty of contacting survivors.

In order to co-ordinate support offered by women's and pro-democracy groups in Jakarta, our initial efforts were centred on establishing links with communities in Chinese-Indonesian neighbourhoods which were most hard-hit by the riots. To ensure we could do this, we held a meeting to organise more volunteers. Around 300 people, men and women, attended the meeting; they were mostly people who had contacted various telephone hotlines opened by NGOs for those who could give information on the rapes, and for the survivors of rape themselves. This mass volunteering was an unprecedented outpouring of support to help survivors of violence against women in Indonesia. A large proportion of volunteers were Chinese-Indonesians; this was also unprecedented. Hitherto, with only a few exceptions, Chinese-Indonesians have chosen to deal with the discrimination they suffer in the Indonesian political system by keeping a low public profile. The public expression of concern and anger about the rapes, and the commitment to work for change, was an important statement on the part of Chinese Indonesians.

The volunteers were then organised into teams in charge of fact-finding, direct support for survivors of rape, and public education on violence against women and racism.

Publicising the rapes: the numbers game

By 2 July 1998, Volunteers for Humanity had documented 168 rapes in Jakarta, Solo, Medan, Palembang and Surabaya. 152 of these occurred in the greater Jakarta area. Some of the victims of rape also suffered other forms of torture, or became trapped in raging fires started by the rioters. Of the 152 women raped, 20 died during or after

Table 1: Number of dead, injured, and disappeared during the mid-May riots.

Date	Number of deaths		Injured		Disappeared	Total
	by weapon	burned	critical	non-critical		
12/5	5		15		1	21
13/5			10			10
14/5		11	19	18		48
15/5	13	458	4		27	502
16/5		146	1		1	148
17/5	4	553			1	559
18/5					1	1
20/5					1	1
24/5		11				11
27/5		5				5
28/5	1		14			15
1/6		6				6
2/6	2	3				5
Total	**25**	**1,193**	**63**	**18**	**32**	**1,332**

the incident. On 17 July, a coalition of women activists, NGOs, intellectuals, and public figures, organised as the Society for the Elimination of Violence Against Women (*Masyarakat Anti Kekerasan terhadap Perempuan*), presented the results of the initial fact-finding to President Habibie. International and national pressure obliged President Habibie to condemn the rapes, and a dialogue between women activists and Habibie resulted in the formation of an investigative team run jointly by the government and NGOs,[3] and headed by the National Commission on Human Rights. Another outcome was the establishment of the National Commission on Violence against Women to address the issue of violence in a more structured and long-term manner.

At the time of writing (October 1998), the accuracy of this report has been questioned; the statistics in it have given rise to reactions including outright denial by government officials. However, in late September this year, the joint government-NGO investigative team confirmed that rapes did take place, although it declined to provide a number for the cases of documented rapes. In the meantime, counter-campaigns denying the accuracy of the reports on rape is gaining momentum in the mainstream press. The continuing denial and counter-campaigns have contributed to an atmosphere of fear and intimidation which is discouraging survivors from coming forward to seek help.

Sexual violence before and beyond the May riots

Since the initial reports on the rapes and other human rights violations in Jakarta, a

Table 2: Chronology of major events leading to the May riots in Indonesia.

1997	
July 97	Economic crisis begins to hit Indonesia, crumbling of the New Order economic miracle.
1998	
January 98	Student protests steadily build momentum throughout Indonesia.
April 98	Riots in Medan, North Sumatra; women students sexually harassed by military forces.
1 May	IMF structural adjustment forces government to stop subsidising fuel, electricity, and basic foods subsidies; prices spiral up, small businesses fold, unemployment is rife in urban areas; students continue to demonstrate.
12 May	Five university students killed by military gunmen; by evening, riots begin.
13 May	**Students buried; riots gain momentum.**
14 May	**Large-scale rioting throughout Jakarta.**
15 May	**Large-scale rioting in Jakarta, Solo, Palembang, and other cities.**
19 May	Suharto calls together community leaders and offers to reshuffle cabinet; students occupy the national parliament building and vow to stay until Suharto steps down; Suharto loyalists in parliament and cabinet call for him to step down.
20 May	Mass demonstration of 1 million people called off by opposition leader due to military pressure.
21 May	Suharto resigns, JB Habibie is sworn in as President.
26 May	First meeting held by women's and volunteer groups to develop a strategy on responses to initial reports of rapes during the May riots.

'domino effect' has occurred. Across the nation, men and women are now speaking out against the atrocities committed by the New Order regime before the unrest. Although Chinese-Indonesian women are a minority group, they are relatively less isolated and marginalised than women from ethnic minorities living in Aceh, East Timor, and Irian Jaya. As a group, Chinese-Indonesians are comparatively well connected with overseas networks, and they have access to greater economic resources than other minority groups who have experienced sexual violence. These are factors which have contributed positively to the build-up of a public outcry. Because the rapes in May occurred at the centre stage of the national scene, where foreign journalists were hungry for a newsworthy story, the atrocities quickly gained national and international attention. This has opened up the way for women from other remote areas to raise their voices and to state that similar atrocities have been happening to them for many years. Stories of torture, rape, and disappearances have surfaced.

Clearly, issues of ethnicity and race are important factors which contributed to these atrocities. The recent rapes in Jakarta grew from an underlying racial discrimination which continues to exist across Indonesia. Women from minority groups are particularly vulnerable to sexual violence — perpetrated by the military, paramilitary forces, or civilian men in powerful positions. In areas where the civilian government takes a back-seat to military rulers, it is a liability to belong to an ethnic group that has challenged the regime. In Aceh, harrowing stories of rape, disappearances, detention, torture and execution are beginning to surface; in East Timor, a women's group is beginning to collect stories of rape and forced labour; in Irian Jaya, indigenous women are providing testimonies on rapes perpetrated by military personnel during operations.

Aceh

Aceh is an oil-rich area with a long history of resistance during the colonial period. Indonesia's western-most province has experienced environmental destruction and unequal economic development. An independence movement has been formed out of popular resentment of the fact that, while the indigenous population are becoming poorer and their environment becomes increasingly degraded, oil companies' employees live in luxury, in enclaves with supermarkets and five-star hotels. Since 1989, Aceh was declared a *daerah operasi militer* (DOM), an area under military authoritarian rule.[4]

A team of members of parliament and NGOs has been formed to document and investigate reports of human rights violations in Aceh. To date, this team,

Table 3: Numbers of documented rapes and sexual harassment in Jakarta, as reported by Volunteers for Humanity, 3 July 1998.

Date	Rape	Rape and torture	Rape and arson	Sexual harassment	Total
13 May		2	3 (3 deaths)	4	9 (3 deaths)
14 May	101	17 (7 deaths)	6 (6 deaths)	8 (1 death)	132 (14 deaths)
15 May		1 (1 death)		1	2 (1 death)
15 May –3 July	2 (1 death)	6 (1 death)		1	9 (2 deaths)
Total	103 (1 death)	26 (9 deaths)	9 (9 deaths)	14 (1 death)	152 (20 deaths)

Data compiled by Volunteers for Humanity, 13 May–3 July 1998.

together with the Indonesian National Human Rights Commission, has documented 781 killings, 163 cases of disappearance, 368 cases of torture, and 102 cases of rape, between 1989-98.[5]

A 42-year-old woman, a villager from Ujong Leubat, Bandar Baru gave a testimony of being raped by three military officers in a military post in Jim Jim in 1992. *'After I was raped, I fainted. In the morning, they kicked me and pushed me into the river. They told me to bathe,'* she said. In 1992 the woman and her husband, Mohamad Yunus, were detained by the Special Forces. They were detained and held in separate rooms. After being raped, the woman was tortured, then released three days later. She never saw her husband again. Afterwards, she heard news of her husband's execution. He was shot with his hands tied to a pole, in front of villagers in Cibrek, Kembang Tanjong.[6]

East Timor

In East Timor, at the beginning of August this year, I assisted a new women's group run a workshop for women who have been affected by the conflict in this territory. Sitting quietly among the older women, whose husbands disappeared or were killed during the war, and among the women survivors of rape and detention, was a 13-year-old girl. She was raped by a military officer in June 1998. Obviously, political change taking place in Jakarta has not reached this part of the world. In this workshop of around 35 people, three out of five children playing in the room were born as a result of rape. The East Timorese women's group, Forum Komunikasi Perempuan Loro Sae (Fokupers), is beginning the slow and painful process of documenting incidents of violence against women.

One woman told her story of being courted and then abandoned by a military officer in 1976. A few years later, she was raped by another soldier after being tied down and hit with a piece of metal. She

was forced to stay in the military complex, cooking, and fetching water and firewood. During this time she was often hit when they thought she was being lazy. If she refused them sex, she would be tied then raped. She bore five children. *'So these are children of war. Before the war I had no children, since the war, I am carrying these children — children of war, children of Indonesia.'* [7]

Irian Jaya/West Papua

From Irian Jaya/West Papua, indigenous women are coming forward with their stories of violence. In Mapenduma, where rebels took hostages and released them after three months in 1997, the military has retaliated in full force. Scores of traditional houses, churches, and villages have been razed to the ground in search of the rebels. In June 1998, church leaders approached the National Human Rights Commission in Jakarta with a report documenting these atrocities. A few months afterwards, human-rights activists have been gathering evidence of rapes which occurred during these raids. Again, incidents of rape are documented as an afterthought, reflecting the male bias in human-rights monitoring instruments. A woman from the Nduga tribe, who live in the highlands of Mapenduma, testified the following to Jayapura-based human-rights workers:

'I was coming home from the field, towards my village, Kuid. I met with military troops on the way. I stepped aside from the path, which is our custom here. We give way to our guests to honour them. They forced me aside. I was raped by seven military men. I was completely helpless and fainted. I became conscious four hours later when some villagers found me and took me home.

'After the freeing of the hostages in Nggeselema, our house was often raided by the military. They wanted me and my daughter to come to the military post. I hid my daughter in the pig sty. One day, they came to ask me to sew some of their clothes. They never paid. I demanded to

be paid, and they gave me bullets. They also destroyed my sewing equipment. I fought back. They stripped me naked and raped me. Somebody took a picture.'[8]

'We want a real live one': media responses to the violence

At the time of writing, a backlash against NGOs which raised the issue of rapes during the May riots is taking shape. Many refuse to accept the truth of the reports, arguing that not a single rape survivor has chosen to provide a public, live testimony, echoing the initial wishes of the press to interview survivors at a time when we were most concerned with protecting victims' confidentiality and supporting them through the crisis.

Meanwhile, continuing intimidation and threats of sexual violence have been levelled towards potential witnesses, including doctors who have testified that they provided treatment to survivors, groups working on this issue, and towards Chinese-Indonesian women in particular, who report increased harassment on the streets. The activities of commercial profiteers and the press have contributed to the normalisation of the threat and reality of sexual violence against women. Advertisements have appeared which promote the age-old idea of chastity belts as 'anti-rape underwear', and the mainstream press has printed countless interviews with the so-called 'inventor'. Recently, a Muslim-based group has taken a weekly magazine to court for allegedly reporting these rapes in a way which degrades Islam.

The Internet has proven to be a tool willing to serve all masters. On the one hand, women's and pro-democracy groups in and outside of Indonesia have made use of the Internet to campaign on this issue. On the other hand, there has also been an effective disinformation campaign using the same medium. Rumours of pending riots and rapes, and false testimonies of such acts, have been widely circulated through the Internet. The fact that this information is false has been taken by some as evidence of the lack of credibility of the groups who are documenting real rapes and working to end such atrocities. Photographs falsely presented as documentation of the May rapes — most of them in fact pictures of torture and rape of women by the military in East Timor — have been downloaded from sites on the Internet. The purpose appears to be disinformation coupled with intimidation. Seeing those pictures makes me feel shocked, personally violated, and disempowered. Can you imagine the effect that they would have on a survivor? The images suggest 'dare you speak, we will do this again'.

The aftermath: campaigning and rehabilitation

Indonesia is entering a time of transition which holds a potential for real change, including change on issues of racism and violence against women. However, this also poses real risks for political disintegration and more violence. Women in Indonesia are playing a major role in organising, testifying, and working for change.

Issues of ethnicity and race continue to play a part in campaigning and rehabilitation work; women's groups which were originally formed to deal with issues of violence against women are learning to incorporate racism into their campaign agenda. Groups in Aceh are asking why there is no international condemnation of the atrocities in Aceh — does this have to do with an anti-Muslim bias in Western media?[9] Most attention (and resources) are still centred on Jakarta. National and international groups concerned with eradicating gender-based violence which are focusing on Indonesia must look at the whole picture, and try to understand the complexities of race, religion, and ethnicity, and how these affect women's experience of gender-based violence.

Future responses must involve multi-ethnic, multi-religious groups and look at the interaction between private and state-supported violence. Focusing interventions on one ethnic group with a particular religion or one geographical area only serves to support the divide-and-rule politics of the New Order regime. Protesting against the rapes of Chinese-Indonesian women without also acknowledging other casualties among the general population which occurred during the riots only serves to isolate the problem and deepen the rift between ethnic groups in this multi-ethnic country. By highlighting the rapes in Jakarta without addressing the same abuses of women from ethnic minorities in faraway places, we are unwittingly guilty of that same racial discrimination. Public pressure must be maintained, and the focus of international and national campaigns must be widened to include rapes in the periphery.

Galuh Wandita works for Yayasan PIKUL, an NGO working on women's health and human rights in Eastern Indonesia, based in Kupang, West Timor. She was a member of the Volunteers for Humanity (Violence Against Women Division) in Jakarta during May-June 1998.
Contact e-mail: gws@kupang.wasantara.net.id

Contact e-mail addresses for relevant organisations:

Volunteers for Humanity, Violence Against Women Division, Jakarta:
galih@indo.net.id
kalyanamitra@nusa.or.id

Mitra Perempuan:
mitraperempuan@iname.com

Flower Aceh:
flower@aceh.wasantara.net.id
Fokupers, Dili, East Timor:
zeus@dili.wasantara.net.id

IHRSTAD, Jayapura:
arrows@mole.gn.apc.org

JKPIT (Eastern Indonesia Women's Health Network), West Timor:
ssp@kupang.wasantara.net.id

Notes

1 At the time, Suharto's New Order regime, alarmed by the extent of public support for the PDI under the leadership of Megawati Sukarnoputri, staged a coup within the PDI and supported a violent take-over of the party by the puppet faction.
2 Witness account in Muara Angke, Jakarta, 14 May 1998, as related in Volunteers for Humanity, Third Documentation Report, July 1998.
3 This team is still conducting its fact-finding mission.
4 Indonesia has three military operations areas: East Timor, Irian Jaya, and Aceh. In August 1998, the Indonesian military commander cancelled Aceh's military operations area status.
5 Report by Fact-Finding Team in Aceh, July 1998, publicised in the national press and disseminated through an Aceh-based news service, Meunasah.
6 Testimony documented by Fact-Finding Team in Aceh, July 1998, disseminated through an Aceh-based internet news service, Meunasah.
7 Testimonies collected by Fokupers as part of their study on the impact of war on women, August 1998 (draft).
8 Statements collected by IHRSTAD, Irian Human Rights Study and Advocacy, in Jayapura, August 1998.
9 Indonesia as a whole is 87 per cent Muslim; Aceh is 99 per cent Muslim.

Reference

Brownmiller S, 'War' in *Against Our Will: Men, women and rape*, 1975.

'I am witness to...':

A profile of Sakshi Violence Intervention Centre in New Delhi, India

Aanchal Kapur

In her work on violence against women, Aanchal Kapur has been inspired by Sakshi, a group working in New Delhi since the early 1990s. In writing this profile of Sakshi, she hopes that others will be inspired, in turn, to join in the struggle against violence. It should become an integral part of networking and advocacy processes — wherever we live and work!

Women all over the world face violence in their daily lives, in ways that have no direct parallels for men. Violence serves the function of maintaining unequal power relations between men and women in society, so our understanding of it cannot be limited either to the personal sphere of family relationships, or to a man-woman relationship. (Kapur 1997) Rather, it must be seen as a reflection of deeper socio-economic processes which are patriarchal[2] in nature.

While violence against women can include physical abuse, psychological abuse, deprivation of resources, and the commodification of women, only the more overt forms of physical violence (especially sexual violence) are widely recognised as 'violence against women'; the more subtle forms are often overlooked. These subtle forms of violence are perpetuated through socio-cultural practices, and the various institutions and systems of society such as family, religion, education, health, economic, legal, political, the media, and the state (including the police and military). Recognising these different manifestations has led some of us to work on the issue, both as individuals and within organisations.

My own work has included conducting workshops on violence and sexuality with college students and women activists; counselling poor women faced with sexual harassment and psychological violence in an urban slum in Delhi; and supporting UNIFEM in planning its activities on violence against women in India, through research, training, advocacy, and lobbying.

In what follows, I share the *profile* of an organisation, and a *process* which has shaped, and continues to shape, my own view of violence against women and children.

The beginnings of Sakshi

Sakshi[3] focuses its work on the issue of violence against women: it aims to create awareness, and promotes justice for women who experience it. It is an effort to intervene and understand the dynamics of violence against women and provides a platform for women to speak out about the violations they face.

Several years ago, Sakshi's founders (Naina Kapur, a lawyer, and Jasjit Purewal, a journalist) began to consider what they could do to confront the silence that shrouds sexual violence[4] in our society. Both women had been addressing violence against women in their respective professions, but a newspaper report of police officers gang-raping a girl in custody triggered off the impetus to channel their work through a formal organisation, which could address violence against women in a concerted way. The case was brought to court and the offenders found guilty. Subsequently, however, the Supreme Court of India reduced the sentence[5] of the offenders by five years, because of the woman's questionable conduct. This case led Naina and Jasjit to question the efficacy of the legal system and the process of justice, and to explore the needs of women at the grassroots who face different forms of sexual violence — which continues to be the more silent and ignored form of assault in India. They realised that children (especially girl children) are the most tragic victims of sexual violence; but in a society which places greater value on female chastity than on a woman's security and freedom, even child victims are forbidden to speak. In fact, any woman who has faced such violence is looked down on by Indian society as having lost her dignity and purity. Because of such beliefs, a woman whose body is violated also risks losing her self-respect and self-esteem in society.

These realities and the deafening silence around the issue finally led to the setting up of Sakshi as an NGO in October 1992, with the aim of opening up a space for speech, expression, and protest on the issue of violence against women, and more specifically on sexual violence.

From the start, Sakshi defined itself as a *'violence intervention centre'*, reflecting its belief that there are many ways in which violence can be prevented. The group wanted to witness, to document, and to enable women to exchange experiences on this all-pervasive form of assault. They adopted a broad definition of violence to include not just physical violence, but also,

more importantly, the subtle forms of mental and emotional violence, including discrimination in the name of 'customs and traditions', and the violence inherent in the socially prescribed status of Indian women.

Today, a multi-disciplinary group of 20 members runs Sakshi. This team includes support staff and professionals from various backgrounds — law, sociology, economics, psychology, journalism, and social work. Many people with different skills (even outside Sakshi) have helped the group in developing their clear idea of what an 'intervention' is with respect to violence. Whether faced with an individual or a system (education, health, judiciary, police, or NGOs), Sakshi's objective has been to make its interventions holistic, long-term, and embracing of difference (of views, contexts, as well as situations). This notion has been tested through various experiences over the years, and time and again continues to be conceptually reviewed.

Sakshi's work has extended into the rural and urban areas of Bihar, Rajasthan, Tamil Nadu, Kerala, Uttar Pradesh; at the national level, it has worked with students, lawyers, judges, police, women's groups, and individual women. Recently, the geographical spread of work has also expanded to some neighbouring South Asian countries, including Nepal, Bangladesh, and Pakistan.

Sakshi's work

Sakshi began its intellectual and action-oriented journey by sharing and learning from experiences on various aspects of violence against women, in workshops with government and non-government organisations all over India. The experiences shared in these workshops demonstrated the 'fear' and loss of 'self-esteem' which violence creates among women. Some workshops[6] started with women's own testimonies, which led to discussions on violence[7;] in other cases, the issue was introduced by discussing concepts of empowerment and gender equality.[8] From the earliest workshops to its present work, Sakshi has tried to make links between violence and women's rights, the law, and strategies for legal change at the local, national, and regional level. Recognising the inter-linkages between different kinds of violence against women, its genesis, and its effects on women's lives, the group has, over the years, developed both short-term and long-term intervention strategies.

The need to research and document women's experiences of violence has led Sakshi to conduct feminist legal research into violations of women's human rights, including women's access to justice, and to create a data bank on different forms of violence against women. Sakshi has also developed training methodologies for making interventions and using the law on this issue. It provides counselling as a specialised service for victims of abuse, especially for children; and has an expanding information-resource base, including simple reference and training material on sexual assault, sexual harassment on the campus, child sexual abuse (CSA)[9], as well as training manuals on gender and judges. These materials can be accessed by interested individuals and organisations for training and advocacy work.

Several projects and programmes have evolved from the above activities. These have ranged from conducting paralegal workshops with women inmates of New Delhi's Tihar prison, to gender-sensitisation training programmes for the police, to research on a gender-based understanding of law in five Indian cities, and programmes of awareness-raising on child sexual abuse[10] among students, counsellors, teachers, parents, police, and the judiciary. Sakshi had also studied the impact of violence on women's mental health with mental health professionals; and investigated linkages between sexual and domestic violence, gender and justice, sex and sexuality among college students.

The Gender and Judges Project

A key programme has been educating members of the judiciary on violence against women through the 'Gender and Judges Project', initiated in 1994. At the start of this project, Sakshi surveyed judicial attitudes to, and perceptions of, violence against women, in order to assess to what extent women's access to justice is restricted as a result of bias in the legal profession. Their 1996 report 'Gender and Judges: A Judicial Point of View' confirmed that there is a pervasive gender bias in the attitudes of judges to violence against women. Simultaneously, it highlighted that 70 per cent of the judges surveyed endorsed the need for gender-equality education. This led to the formation of the 'Asia Pacific Advisory Forum on Judicial Education on Equality Issues', which aims to build capacities of members of the judiciary, through training programmes in different parts of that region, and to ensure that the legal system in each country moves beyond a *principle* of equality to *actually* treating women equally with men. The Gender and Judges Project has also been very well received in Nepal, Bangladesh, and Pakistan, and Sakshi's inputs have catalysed local groups to start independent work on these issues.

The Supreme Court Guidelines on Sexual Harassment at the Workplace[11]

Sakshi has been involved in lobbying for the issue of sexual harassment at work to be addressed in the Indian legal system for the past few years. For the first time in India, the Supreme Court passed a set of Guidelines on Sexual Harassment at the Workplace in August 1997.[12] These are the outcome of a long struggle, triggered off as a protest against the continued harassment of a woman development worker in Bhateri, a village in Rajasthan.

The woman, who was working for the Government's Women's Development Programme, trying to stop child marriages in upper-caste households, faced repeated sexual harassment in her work. Her complaints to the local authorities drew a blank and no inquiry or investigation took place. Eventually, she was gang-raped in front of her husband's eyes in 1991. Women's groups from all over the country came together in solidarity to protest against this abuse of the human rights of a woman development worker. In addition to the criminal case for rape, Sakshi, together with other social activists, filed a legal petition with the Supreme Court of India, demanding the establishment of guidelines prohibiting sexual harassment in the workplace as a woman worker's right.

According to these Guidelines, sexual harassment is defined as any unwelcome physical contact and advances, requests for sexual favours, sexual innuendo, display of pornography, and any other unwelcome physical, verbal, or non-verbal conduct of a sexual nature. The Guidelines emphasise the need for preventive action apart from addressing individual complaints, and expand the understanding of sexual harassment as a violation of human rights, instead of treating it as a criminal offence only. In addition to preventive and criminal law remedies, the Court has also stressed the need for awareness-raising at the workplace among the employers and the employees.

Until necessary legislation is passed, these Guidelines are legally binding and enforceable. All government and private-sector organisations, hospitals, universities, and other responsible persons, and the informal sector, come under the purview of the guidelines. Women who either draw a regular salary, receive an honorarium, or work in a voluntary capacity, will benefit from these guidelines. All employers or responsible heads of institutions are supposed to institute rules governing their employees' behaviour, and preventive measures to stop sexual harassment.

The Guidelines are to be implemented by setting up a complaints committee within each organisation, of which half the members are women and which is headed by a woman. In order to prevent undue pressure from within the organisation, the committee is to include a third-party representative from an NGO or any other body conversant with the issue of sexual harassment.

The judgement establishing these Guidelines has not only brought to the fore the issue of sexual harassment at work, but has also led to an increased level of awareness-raising, organising, research, and training on issues of violence against women, both in public and private organisations in India. Sakshi has also started to run training sessions on how to use the Guidelines in different organisations from the government, the private, and the informal sector, and in universities. It is hoped that these capacity-building and advocacy measures will make the guidelines a reality, and that they will take on legislative status in the coming years.

Challenges facing Sakshi

One of the main challenges for Sakshi has been to work towards an inclusive process of knowledge-building and sharing, as well as maintaining its process-oriented focus, while recognising the need to institution-alise its approach to deal with violence interventions. This need to share its growing knowledge and experience, and learn from others, has led the organisation to network with a wide variety of individuals, government, and non-government organisations, as well as with bilateral and multi-lateral agencies.

A second major challenge for Sakshi has been, and continues to be, the search for funds to support its work. Sakshi's eventual aim is to be free from donor dependency and to create its own core fund. However, in the meantime funding must be sought from development donors. While some agencies have provided resources for specific projects, it has not been easy to negotiate continuous support for its research and capacity-building agenda, which emphasises the importance of process, a holistic view, and sustainability.

In my experience, Sakshi's dilemmas on this issue are shared by many other NGOs today, and are the result of changes in development financing in recent years, which has meant more project-based funding, and less institutional or issue-based funding. It is important to understand that 'ending violence' is not a 'tangible deliverable' as required by some donors, and this impinges on the availability of funds. Therefore, a certain amount of creative 'social marketing' of the issue seems to be the need of the hour! Working with international donors is a topic which demands an article in itself, and there is little room to debate it here, but one needs to note that, in the past five years, international agencies have been setting their own development agendas for a particular country, rather than allowing development to be a *demand-driven* and *needs-based* process. This has also, inevitably, led to institutional changes at local level — for example, the mushrooming of NGOs whose activities match donor agendas — and to a reduction of funds available to existing groups to sustain work on issues to which they are committed in the long-term. I raise this point here in the hope that it will stimulate future debate among readers of this article.

Looking to the future

Experience over the years has led Sakshi to realise that 'violence cannot be countered by intervention measures alone... for maximum effectivity we needed to link our campaigns against violence with other forms of gender development'[13] (Annual Report 1996–97). Six years after its inception, the Sakshi team wishes to consolidate this understanding, and is therefore using the concept of '*substantive equality*' (meaning *de facto* equality) in order to strategise for change. This concept is expected to help form the links between different systems in society and to enhance different people's vision of work on violence interventions, whether they are judges, lawyers, teachers, social activists, doctors, or psychiatrists. In order to work towards constructive change, Sakshi's has therefore initiated dialogues with various systems like the judiciary, educators and the academia, medical professionals, and other NGOs.[14] A second concept that Sakshi has taken from its experiences of working with women in situations of violence is the importance of 'informed choice'. The absence of this choice is the most consistent obstacle to a woman's sense of her rights, of her quest for justice (personal or institutional) and of herself as a human being. Thus, Sakshi is constantly reaffirming the need for educating societal institutions on the concept of 'informed choice', so as to advocate measures of support consistent with an understanding of a woman's social context. This is also necessary for empowering women to demand and exercise this choice in times of need.

As I conclude, I hope that readers of this journal will support the work of Sakshi and other like-minded organisations, which have taken on the responsibility of being witnesses to all kinds of violence against women and children — a responsibility which needs to be shared by many more organisations than it is at present. I hope that, together, we can find creative ways of sensitising and capacity-building on an issue which denies women their human right to life without fear and shame.

Aanchal Kapur is an action-researcher and trainer on women's issues who has worked with NGOs and other development agencies in India for the past eight years. Using information as a source of communication and networking, inside and outside of India, is of particular interest to her. She also is co-ordinator of the Women Workers' Rights Project at the International Labour Organisation in New Delhi. She can be contacted at: Block III/78 (F.F.), Sunshine Avenue, Charmwood Village, Eros Gardens, New Delhi 110 044; Tel: +91 (129) 251006/251047, E-mail:aanchal@sapta.com

Sakshi is located at: B-67 (F.F.), South Extension -I, New Delhi 110 049; Tel/Fax: (91) (11) 4643926 E-mail:sakdel@irc.unv.ernet.in

Notes

1 This article has been written with inputs of different members of the Sakshi team including Naina Kapur, Jasjit Purewal, Nandita Baruah, Maya Ganesh, Geeta, and others. I would also like to thank Sital Kalantry and Vidya for their support.

2 The causes of violence can be traced to patriarchy, which is manifest in society in different ways. Patriarchy as an ideology is reflected through men's control and domination of women (Kriti, 1993). It accords the male gender a superior status over women, and enables men to claim all avenues of power. Patriarchy is perpetuated through social, cultural, and religious practices, and legitimised through the political, legal, educational, medical, and economic systems of society. Thereby, patriarchy controls women's fertility, sexuality, labour mobility, and access to resources at the material and ideological levels.

3 Sakshi is the Hindi term for 'witness'.

4 One of its earliest booklets, 'Have you been Sexually Assaulted?' has been translated into 12 languages and is used in training programmes all over India.

5 The maximum sentence for rape under Indian law is between seven and ten years, so these offenders got away with considerably less.

6 The different approaches have been used both with local women and with activists/workers, depending on their level of awareness and skills.

7 For example, a workshop with 50 women in rural Bihar started with women sharing their own experiences of sexual violence and was followed by the Sakshi team clarifying concepts about women's sexuality and violence.

8 Such a workshop was held with tribal women in Rajasthan. It began by examining the concept of empowerment, which women felt from their political and economic struggle for control of their land, and then moved on to the unexplored terrain of discussing honour and morality associated with violence.

9 Sakshi has done intensive research into CSA, leading to the development of a comprehensive learning package, which comprises counselling casework, research, and awareness-raising workshops. At present, it is also looking at the issue from a mental health perspective.

10 Sakshi's unpublished research with school children, on the issue of CSA has shown a 23 per cent incidence of hard-spectrum abuse.

11 Judgement dated 13 August 1997, passed by the Supreme Court of India in a case titled, 'Vishaka & Others *vs* State of Rajasthan & Others', Writ Petition (Criminal) Nos 666-70 of 1992.

12 Although the guidelines still do not meet all our expectations, we see them as a positive first step in the direction of recognising and dealing with the issue.

13 This recognition has also established the need for Sakshi to mainstream its understanding and intervention strategies to make the required impact in society.

14 The dialogue has been made informative and creative by the use of theatre, dance, puppetry, experiential exercises, films, and tele-conferencing.

'Circumcision', culture, and health-care provision in Tower Hamlets, London

Joan Cameron and Karen Rawlings Anderson

Tower Hamlets has a sizeable Somali community, who maintain close links to their culture and country of origin. About 80 per cent of Somali women are estimated to have undergone 'female circumcision'. The authors carried out research to assess whether British health services meet Somali women's health-care needs. Interestingly, they found that reasons given to justify female circumcision mirror those used in the UK to justify episiotomy in childbirth.

There is overwhelming evidence that female 'circumcision' endangers women's health, and confers no physical benefit on the woman or her children. It has been widely condemned by health-care professionals throughout the world. However, we argue in this article that, because health-care professionals concentrate on the biological effects of the practice rather than on understanding its cultural context, health-care professionals are perceived by women who have undergone circumcision as taking a judgemental stance towards the communities in which female circumcision is practised. There is evidence that this may alienate individual members of those communities and inhibit women who have undergone circumcision from accessing health services.

This is ironic, because there is a parallel between reasons given by health-care professionals in Britain to justify the widespread practice of episiotomy in childbirth, and those offered for female circumcision by the Somali community. Both practices are seen as necessary for women's good health in a specific cultural context. We make suggestions for improving health-service provision in future for Somali women in Tower Hamlets, emphasising the importance of community participation in health-care planning.

First, a note on terminology. The practice referred to in this article is most commonly known as 'female genital mutilation'. This indicates that the practice is harmful, and it is the terminology most often used by health-care professionals in Britain and by activists working on the issue as an abuse of women's human rights. However, in this article we have chosen to use the term 'female circumcision' — not because these perspectives are wrong, but because many Somali women in Tower Hamlets told us that they found the term 'mutilation' stigmatising and alienating; they prefer the term 'circumcision'. The conversations with Somali women which form the basis of this article were held in the context of collaborative work between the authors and the London Black Women's Health Action Group, with the aim of obtaining funding for a health clinic for Somali women.

The context of the study

Tower Hamlets is an inner-city area in London, Great Britain. The area is one of the most deprived in England (ELCHA, 1997) with high levels of unemployment and overcrowding. Tower Hamlets has a diverse population, which includes a growing Somali community, estimated to be approximately 10,000 (ELCHA, 1995); however, reliable statistics about the size of the Somali community in Tower Hamlets are not available. Estimations of populations are based on census figures, which do not reflect country of origin. Many people of Somali origin living in Tower Hamlets are refugees, who have come to live in the area since the last census.

The London Black Women's Health Action Project (LBWHAP) is a not-for-profit organisation which was established by a group of women in Tower Hamlets in 1982. It is the main point of contact for Somali women in east London who want to obtain information about health issues. A recent study by LBWHAP in 1993 found that the majority of the Somali community in Tower Hamlets arrived quite recently, and many of them still have strong links with their families in Somalia.

What is 'female circumcision'?

Female circumcision is a name given to a practice (or, more correctly, practices) carried out in many countries, predominately in Africa and the Middle East. The practice is popularly associated with several religions, but there is no substantive evidence that it is a requirement of any religion. Dorkenoo (1994) suggests that female circumcision is endorsed by some religious leaders as a way of continuing the subjugation of women in society. It is practised by Muslims, Christians, and other faiths, but it is most closely associated with the Islamic faith.

The most prevalent practices are described briefly here. Clitoridectomy involves the partial or total removal of the clitoris. Excision involves removing the clitoris along with part or all of the labia minora. The upper part of the vulval area is then stitched, and becomes scarified. Infibulation, the most radical practice, involves excising the clitoris, labia minora, and labia majora. Afterwards the region is sutured, so that only a small hole is left for menstruation and urination. This procedure results in the formation of extensive scar tissue (Flannery et al, 1990). Excision is the most common type of circumcision performed world-wide, but infibulation is the most common procedure in Somalia; this pattern is true of the Somali community living in Tower Hamlets.

It is estimated that over 80 per cent of all Somali women are infibulated (Black and Debelle, 1998). The procedure can be carried out at any age, but it is most commonly performed on children between the ages of five and 12 (Dirie and Lindmark, 1991). Although the practice is illegal in Britain, there is some evidence to suggest that the practice of infibulation does happen in Britain; it is either performed by traditional attendants, or in some cases by registered medical practitioners (Dyer, 1993). It has also been reported that some girls are returned to Somalia to be circumcised (Black and Debelle, 1998)

Reasons given for the practice

Female circumcision is a harmful practice which confers no biological benefit to women. However, it is perceived by many within the communities in which it is practised to confer benefits, including health-related ones. Depending on the cultural context, research has shown that there are a variety of different reasons cited for the practice. These include reducing female sexual desire as a means of maintaining chastity, virginity, and fidelity, and also as a way of increasing male sexual pleasure (Direi and Lindmark 1991; Ebong, 1997). The practice is also regarded as a form of initiation into womanhood, and a means of ensuring social cohesion and integration. In many communities, an uncircumcised woman is considered to be unmarriageable (Shorten, 1995). Female circumcision may also take place because the female genitals are considered unsightly, and the practice is seen as enhancing the aesthetic appeal of women (Spadacini and Nichols, 1998).

Other reasons for female circumcision are health-related, including the belief that female genitalia are unhygenic, and that circumcision will reduce body odour (Grassivaro-Gallo and Viviani, 1992). It is sometimes thought that circumcision enhances fertility, while others believe that the labia will carry on growing if they are not excised (Slack, 1988). Another health reason cited for the circumcision of women is the belief that the baby will die at birth if the clitoris touches the baby's head (Kouba and Muasher, 1985). In the Tower Hamlets community, Somali women and men who spoke to the LBWHAP confirmed such beliefs, and prioritised tradition and religious obligations as the main reasons for the practice. Protection of virginity and control of female sexual desire where also cited as rationales. Many respondents also stated that uncircumcised females were not accepted, because people regard them as bringing shame by disrespecting their cultural traditions and customs.

The impact on women's health

In Tower Hamlets, as in the rest of the UK, most of our knowledge about the health-care needs of circumcised women is based on medical research which typically focuses on medical or obstetric problems and deinfibulation (see below for a definition). Physical health complications associated with infibulation in particular are very severe (Arbesman, Kahler and Buck, 1991), while many women and girl children undoubtedly suffer severe psychological scars as a result of undergoing all forms of circumcision. In particular, infibulation directly impacts on gynaecological, genito-urinary, and obstetric health. For example, cervical smears may be difficult or impossible to carry out, so routine screening for cervical cancer cannot occur. Infibulated women giving birth vaginally may require extensive perineal surgery to facilitate the birth of the baby. However, infibulation also affects women indirectly: for example, in an emergency situation such as cardiac collapse or renal failure, urinary catheterisation (where a tube is passed through the urethral opening into the bladder) is required to monitor urinary output. For a woman who has been infibulated, urethral catheterisation may be impossible, and the more complex and invasive procedure of supra-pubic catheterisation may be required (this involves making an incision in the abdomen and inserting a tube into the bladder).

The immediate complications of infibulation include severe pain and bleeding, leading to shock. Infection may ensue as the instruments used for the procedure are frequently not sterile. Urinary retention may also result because the woman or child is reluctant to urinate to avoid the pain of urine touching raw tissue. Of the 200 women in the LBWAP survey in Tower Hamlets, 61 per cent were infibulated by people with no medical training. More than half of the infibulated women reported suffering haemorrhage, urinary retention, and infection as a result of the operation.

A number of long-term complications as a result of infibulation have been reported (Calder, Brown and Rae, 1993; Dirie and Lindmark, 1992; Shorten, 1995). These include dysmenorrhoea (painful menstruation) and recurrent urinary problems because the perineal opening is too small to allow the escape of menstrual blood and urine. Efua Dorkenoo (1994) reports that some women have such small perineal openings that the flow of menstrual blood is impeded to such an extent that the abdomen becomes distended. This has led to some young women being killed to preserve the family's honour. Fistulae (abnormal openings between the bladder and vagina, or between the bladder and rectum), cysts, and abscess formation, and damage to the urethra which leads to incontinence, can follow as a result of difficulties caused by infibulation during childbirth. Ten per cent of the women surveyed by LBWHAP in Tower Hamlets reported suffering urethral damage as a result of infibulation which continued to cause them urinary incontinence. Dyspareunia (painful intercourse) is common due to vaginal atrophy (shrinkage) as a result of the infibulation; dyspareunia is also likely if vaginal penetration is attempted without deinfibulation.

The practice of removing stitches and scar tissue to 're-open' the vaginal opening — referred to as 'deinfibulation' is traditionally carried out at the time of marriage or childbirth. Deinfibulation is commonly performed by cutting with a blade or other sharp instrument. This can expose the women to further risks such as infection and bleeding. Almost 80 per cent of the infibulated women reported being frightened and nervous during their first weeks of marriage due to the effects of infibulation.

Health-care responses to female 'circumcision'

In contrast to the detailed picture of the medical and obstetric effects of infibulation given in the previous section, we know very little about the expectations of women in regard to health-care services, and we know little about their specific health-care needs. The major non-medical focus on female circumcision in the UK has been on protecting girl children from undergoing the practice. Whilst progress in this area is obviously of paramount importance for the well-being of future generations, the needs of women who have already been circumcised have received scant attention, with the exception of isolated services providing 'deinfibulation' under safe medical conditions (MacCaffery, Jankowska and Gordon, 1995). Even if the practice of female circumcision were stopped tomorrow, in Tower Hamlets alone, a significant number of circumcised women in need of health-care provision would remain.

Information about the incidence of female circumcision already existing within the population is not routinely collected by health-care agencies, including hospitals and general practitioners (family doctors), so it is difficult to assess the numbers of women affected. However, the fact that in 1994-95, LBWHAP received 792 phone calls, indicates that there is a significant number of Somali women who wish to gain access to health-related information and services. Since a delay in responding to the health-care needs of a woman who has undergone circumcision may compromise the health — or life — of a woman or her baby, it is critical that information about female circumcision is collected as part of routine health assessments.

As stated earlier, health-care provision for circumcised women in Tower Hamlets mainly focuses on deinfibulation. There is a community clinic, where the procedure can be carried out on an out-patient basis, or women can go to Northwick Park Hospital's African Well Women Clinic. However, disseminating information on deinfibulation services is essential, because women will not make use of a service if they do not know it exists. Anecdotal evidence suggests that there is ignorance among health-care professionals about the possibility of deinfibulation and the existence of the clinics; they assume that women are infibulated for life.

Regarding the mental health of women who have undergone circumcision, at the moment voluntary organisations such as LBWHAP provide support to women in whose area they work. In Tower Hamlets, many Somali women also have to deal with a wider context of poverty and racism. These factors alone are associated with adverse mental and physical health outcomes (ELCHA, 1996). It is unacceptable for voluntary organisations to be the sole support for a significant proportion of the community, particularly when their health-care needs are likely to be long-standing. Typically, financial constraints limit the scope and duration of voluntary support.

Until information about Somali women's health-care needs is collected systematically and directly from the community itself, inappropriate services will continue to be provided. One possible approach to resolve the lack of information from the community and the perceived gap in service provision could be to undertake systematic research locally. This kind of research is essential because of the difficulty in generalising information from other areas to Tower Hamlets. The experience and knowledge base of local voluntary organisations such as LBWHAP must be acknowledged by researchers and health-care providers whichever approach is chosen.

Ways forward

This paper was intended to make the case for the provision of appropriate health services for circumcised women in Tower Hamlets. In line with Government health policy, we have argued that this cannot be achieved without community participation in health-care planning.

The UK Government has recently published a White Paper, 'The New NHS Modern Dependable' (Department of Health, 1997), which emphasises the need for health-care professionals to work in partnership with local communities to shape local health services. In the case of Tower Hamlets, we envisage future research which would go some way to realising this need. In collaboration with LBWHAP, we have proposed a study to assess the expressed health-care needs of circumcised Somali women. The proposed project would analyse the match between health-care provision and the wishes of users, and would provide information to the health authority on the needs of its local population, focusing on a group who have previously been marginalised, stigmatised, and who have had little voice in service planning.

In addition, given the emotive nature of female circumcision, it is important to establish what existing knowledge, skills, and attitudes health-care professionals possess in relation to the practice and their clients. Obvious professional groups to include in this part of the study would be midwives, gynaecology and sexual health nurses, practice nurses, general practitioners, obstetricians, and gynaecologists. In addition, health-care professionals from other specialised areas may have contact with women who have experienced circumcision, and it is proposed that they should also be included in the survey.

Parallels with 'Western' practices

One way of challenging British health-care professionals to examine their own attitudes to the culture of communities where female circumcision exists is to argue that practices affecting the female genitalia are not restricted to those communities. There are, in fact, parallels within Western health-care, where some practices are used inappropriately, and health-care professionals formulate justifications for common interventions in spite of evidence that they may be harmful. One example is that of episiotomy, a surgical incision of the perineum to enlarge the vaginal outlet performed during childbirth.

Episiotomy was virtually unknown before this century. It was originally used in Western Europe and North America to facilitate births where forceps were to be used. Subsequently, as most women ceased to give birth at home but routinely went into hospital, episiotomy became a routine procedure (Thacker and Banta, 1983). A study by Murphy Black in 1989 found that 87 per cent of all women having their first babies in one hospital were given an episiotomy and 27 per cent of women having third babies had an episiotomy. However, evidence suggests that the episiotomy rate should be less than 20 per cent (Sleep et al, 1984).

In 1995, an attempt by the Association for Improvements in Maternity Services to have episiotomy labelled as genital mutilation was greeted with outrage (Beech, 1994). Midwives stated that, far from being an unnecessary practice which constitutes violence against women, the procedure was a necessary health intervention and was used only when indicated. A number of benefits have been attributed to episiotomy (Thacker and Banta, 1983; Sleep et al, 1984): it has been claimed that it prevents damage to the rectal mucosa and anal sphincter; that a cut is easier to repair than a tear, and that an episiotomy wound will heal faster than a tear. It has also been suggested that the procedure prevents trauma to the foetal head during delivery.

However, Sleep et al in 1984 found that episiotomy did not prevent tears, nor did the wounds caused by the practice heal faster than tears. Episiotomy did not appear to have a protective effect on the pelvic floor, and did not prevent incontinence (Sleep et al, 1984). Lobb et al (1986), investigating the role of episiotomy in protecting the baby's head during birth, found that it did not influence the incidence of intracranial bleeds (bleeding into the brain) in premature babies. All the adverse after-effects experienced by women who have undergone female circumcision have been reported as the outcomes of episiotomy and subsequent repair (Wagner 1994). It is clear that the indiscriminate use of episiotomy is justified by health-care professionals who construct their own explanations to convince themselves and their clients of its benefits, in spite of evidence to the contrary.

Conclusion

As health-care providers, we are arguing that understanding the practices widely known as female genital mutilation from the perspective of women who have undergone it is essential for the provision of appropriate health services. Communities should be involved in the planning of these services. Understanding the context in which the practices exist does not mean rejecting the perspective that such practices are harmful for women. However, stigmatising women who have already undergone circumcision could be avoided if health-care professionals in the UK context recognise that these practices do not only occur in the context of 'other' cultures. Episiotomy parallels the practice of female circumcision, because evidence that the practice is harmful is countered by strong health-related, as well as cultural, arguments for its continuance; any attempt to change attitudes among health-care professionals to circumcised women in the UK must acknowledge this.

Joan Cameron is a Lecturer in Neonatal Care and Midwifery, City University, London.
Karen Rawlings Anderson is a Senior Lecturer in Adult Nursing, City University, London. Address for correspondence: City University School of Nursing & Midwifery, Philpot Street, London E1 2EA, UK.

References

Arbesman, M, Kahler, L and Buck, G (1993) 'Assessment of the gynaecological, genitourinary and obstetrical health problems of women in Somalia: literature review and case series', *Women and Health* 20(3) 27–42.

Beech B (1994) 'Episiotomy: Female Genital Mutilation', *AIMS Quarterly Journal* Summer pp 1–2.

Black, JA and Debelle, GD (1998) 'Female genital Mutilation in Britain', *British Medical Journal* 310 (6994) 1590–1594.

Calder, BL, Brown, YM and Rae, DI (1993) 'Female circumcision/genital mutilation: culturally sensitive care', *Health Care For Women International* 14(3) 227–238.

Department of Health (1997) *The new NHS Modern Dependable* Cmnd 3807 London: The Stationary Office.

Dirie, MA and Lindmark, G (1992) 'Female circumcision in Somalia and women's motives', *Acta Obstetrica et Gynaecological Scandinavia* 70, 581–585.

Dirie, MA and Lindmark, G (1992) 'The risk of medical complications after female circumcision', *East African Medical Journal* 69(9) 479–482.

Dorkenoo, E (1994) *Cutting the Rose: Female Genital Mutilation — The Practice and its Prevention*, London: Minority Rights Publications.

Dyer, O (1993) 'Gynaecologist struck off over female circumcision', *British Medical Journal* 307 (6917) 1441–1442.

East London and The City Health Authority (ELCHA) (1995) *Health in the East End, Annual Public Health Report 1995/6* London; The Directorate of Public Health, ELCHA.

East London and The City Health Authority (ELCHA) (1997) *Health in the East End Annual Public Health Report 1997/8*. London; The Directorate of Public Health, ELCHA.

Ebong, R (1997) 'Female circumcision and its health implications: a study of the Urban Local Government Area of Akwa Ibom State, Nigeria', *Journal of the Royal Society of Health* 117(2) 95–99.

Flannery, MS; Glover, ED and Airhinenbuwa, C (1990) *Health Values: Achieving High Level Wellness* 14(5) 34–40.

Grassivaro Gallo, P and Viviani, F (1992) ,The origin of infibulation in Somalia: an ethnological hypothesis', *Ethnology and Socio-biology* 13 253–265.

Kouba, LJ & Muasher, J (1985) 'Female circumcision in Africa: an overview', *African Studies Review* 28(1) 95–110.

Lobb M, Duthie SJ and Cooke RWI (1986) 'The influence of episiotomy on the neonatal survival and incidence of periventriclar haemorrhage in very low birth weight infants', *European Journal of Obstetrical, Gynaecological and Reproductive Biology*, 22 pp 17–21.

London Black Women's Health Action Project (1993) *Attitudes and views of East Africa Women and Men on Female Genital Mutilation*, London: LBWHAP.

McCaffrey, M; Jankowska, A, and Gordon, H (1995) 'Management of Female Genital Mutilation: the Northwick Park Experience', *British Journal of Obstetrics and Gynaecology* 102, 787–790.

Murphy Black, T (1989 *Postnatal care at Home: A descriptive Study of Mothers' Needs and the Maternity Services*, Edinburgh, University of Edinburgh.

Shorten, A (1995) 'Female circumcision: understanding special needs', *Holistic Nursing Practice* 9(2) 66–73.

Slack, A (1988) 'Female circumcision: a critical appraisal', *Human Rights Quarterly* 10 437–486.

Sleep J, Grant A et al (1984) West Berkshire Perineal Management Trial. *British Medical Journal* 289, pp 587–590

Spadacini and Nichols (1998).

Wager M (1995) *Pursuing the Birth Machine*. Australia, Ace Graphics.

Political change, rape, and pornography in post-apartheid South Africa

Teboho Maitse

Maitse argues that in post-apartheid South Africa, perceptions of what it means to be a woman are changing. Men are finding it difficult to adapt to these changes and, fuelled by the ready availability of pornography, are reacting with increased rape and violence against women.

There are periods in history when fundamental changes take place. By the end of the twentieth century, democratic governments will lead many countries in Africa, and this will be referred to as a positive, as well as an historic, change. But there are many definitions of democracy, and many views on how this democracy affects men and women. Tied to this are notions of masculinity and femininity, as these are outcomes of history. South Africa currently has a higher representation of women in Parliament — 25 per cent — than any other Commonwealth country, except the Seychelles. Yet male violence against women has assumed new proportions. In this article, I argue that in South Africa the paradigms of what it is to be a woman are changing, and men find it difficult to accept the change: hence the high incidence of violence and rape, fuelled by the ready availability of pornography.

Violence against women in South Africa

In the 'new' South Africa, women are still raped, molested, and humiliated, despite the fact that we have one of the most progressive constitutions in the world. According to media reports, at least 62 women were raped in the Johannesburg area in the first three weeks of June 1998 (Saturday Star, 27 June 1988). Police stated that the actual figure would be higher, because it is estimated that only one in 36 rapes is reported. This means that another 2,000 women probably suffered the same fate over this period. The same report informs us that while 'as many as 30 per cent of men rape women in the rapist's own home, 29 per cent rape in open areas and 14 per cent in the women's home'. The report confirms the commonly held view that women are often assaulted by people whom they know rather than by strangers: 'In 46 per cent of reported rapes the women knew their attacker by sight. And although three of five rape survivors have never seen their attacker before, it is very likely that many of those who know their rapists do not report the attack' (ibid).

There is nothing new about woman-battering or sexual violence against women in South Africa; throughout history, South African women have been subjected to the whims and brutality of men. Male violence towards women has always been accepted as a natural if unfortunate part of women's status as men's property (Maitse 1997). In answer to the question why men are violent towards women in the context of South Africa, two primary inter-connected theories emerge. The first is that of sexist ideology, and men's preoccupation with all the qualities assigned to the male sex role. The second theory draws a shocking picture of South African society as a 'rape culture', in which violence against women is tacitly accepted. Evidence for this theory is provided by women's experiences of violence at the hands of the institutions which run society, for example, the police; and it is indicated by the great importance that society attaches to male power and aggression, as well as to the social factors which lead to violence.

Before apartheid ended, violence against women, particularly violence against women which occurred within the seclusion of the home, was not deemed a criminal offence. The violence was reinforced by the ethos of apartheid in general and the perception that apartheid had denuded African men of their authority over women (according to the law, African men's status was inferior to that of white women). In addition, the regime's theory that African men were the most violent members of society made it possible for violence to continue, without any significant objections being raised by state or society (Maitse 1997).

In addition to these theories, there is a common, and problematic, link made between male violence and poverty (CIET Survey 1998). Male violence is associated with the country's political and social transition, since the change has increased some men's sense of insecurity. I argue that this explanation of violence displays the self-interest and biased interpretations of those who control the gathering and dissemination of information (Spender 1982). Using theories of social deprivation

to explain crimes against women results in projecting blame onto an abstract, albeit genuine, reality, rather than placing responsibility with the perpetrator. The rationalisation that crimes against women are a by-product of social deprivation is not rooted in historical reality — men have been assigned the ultimate power and authority over women from time immemorial. Women are not exempt from poverty — in fact, they are the poorest of all people in this country; yet they do not rape or commonly commit violent acts against people. Most critically, using poverty to explain men's violence towards women risks excusing the violence, and does not force men to take responsibility for their actions.

For the majority of South African women, the concept of 'home' has a deceptive dual meaning: on the one hand, it is a sanctuary, haven, and place of safety; and on the other, it is a potential prison and torture chamber (Hamner 1989). The home is a site for individual men to oppress women in their own particular way. Here, men have the freedom to do what they like to women (Campbell 1992). This is where pornography plays a major part, because some men find the sexual violence and aggression induced by pornography erotic and desirable (Russell 1993).

There is a general reluctance among women in general, and among both women and men working for development organisations and other NGOs, to discuss the harmfulness of pornography, and a lack of understanding that there is a connection between pornography and all forms of violence against women. A study I carried out in 1993–94 revealed the clear links between pornography and violence against women. Of the 74 women interviewed, 20 claimed that their partners had access to pornographic material; they were often forced to emulate some of the pornographic images, and when they refused to do so, they were assaulted (Maitse 1997). In addition to my own study, there is considerable other evidence to suggest that pornography harms women in a wide range of ways, directly — emotionally by being forced to view it, and physically by being forced to copy it — or indirectly, for example, when women undergo assaults inspired by it (Itzin, 1992).

This silence on the part of organisations is particularly worrying to those whose objective is to sensitise the public conscience about the problem of male violence towards women. Ironically, we do not seem so doubtful about making a link between pornographic pictures of children and child sexual abuse. Recently, nude pictures of children at an arts festival in Grahamstown, South Africa, elicited a lot of debate about the association of pornography with child sexual abuse. I suppose that people's silence on the connections between pornography and abuse of women is induced by the fear that discussing pornography would make us confront and need to understand the contempt that some men have for women. Pornography is designed as an accessory to help men masturbate, and the pleasure of ejaculation becomes associated with the degrading depictions of women, which is ultimately harmful to both men and women.

Pornography and 'rights'

South Africans currently have easy access to pornography. The open availability of pornography, be it on the top shelves of newsagents or on street corners, advocates hatred towards women. Seven days a week and all day long, women's naked bodies and vaginas are publicly displayed for visual rape. The use of pornography in South Africa is not a new phenomenon; but it is now legal, and easily accessible.

At the time of my own study in 1993–94, pornography was illegal. Before the advent of the new democracy, the Publication and Entertainment Act of 1963 and the Publication Act of 1979 prohibited the sale or possession of pornography, although it was in fact available. Based on the discoveries in my study, I have concluded that the prohibition of pornography did not actually protect women, since men were still able to gain access to pornographic material. Its illegal status simply meant that the state could conserve the image of family and Christian values which, at the time, supposedly guided South Africa's governance.

In contrast, under the new Constitution, violent and degrading images of women are legally condoned through the 'freedom of expression' clauses in the Bill of Rights — despite the fact that the new South African Constitution explicitly provides the protection of each individual's human rights. Among other rights, our constitution states that everyone has inherent dignity, and the right to have their dignity respected and protected. Furthermore, the Bill of Rights maintains that this subsection does not advocate the right to 'incitement of imminent violence; or advocacy of hatred that is based on race, ethnicity, gender or religion and that constitutes incitement to cause harm' (Constitution of the Republic of South Africa 1996, Act 108 of 1996). It is unfortunate that this right does not protect women from sexist and demeaning imagery in the form of pornography, because the constitution also protects people's freedom of artistic expression. The Constitution also states that every person has the right to freedom of expression, which includes freedom of the press and other media; and that everyone has the right to 'freedom of artistic creativity' (ibid). This conflict between protecting human rights and ensuring creative freedom remains to be addressed; indeed, it is doubtful whether it can be resolved.

Government action and legislation

There are some positive signs that the issue of violence against women is being addressed; it has emerged as a priority for action by government and many NGOs. The South African Government has committed itself to eradicating violence against women, and has stated that it intends to comply with the provisions of the Beijing Platform for Action.

Furthermore, it has ratified the Convention on the Elimination of All Forms of Discrimination Against Women (CEDAW). To fulfil this decree the government passed the Domestic Violence Bill (Legi-Link Profiles, Bill no B75-88, 20 July 1998). In legal terms, the Bill provides for the granting of protection orders in cases of domestic violence; for an obligation to report cases of suspected ill-treatment of children; for a criminal conviction of a husband who rapes; and for matters connected therewith. The Bill recognises that 'controlling or abusive behaviour that harms the health, safety or well-being of the woman or child… emotional, verbal and psychological abuse together with other forms of abuse' (ibid), directed at women, denies them their basic human rights.

However, in my analysis, the Bill is flawed. It fails to address the issue of escalating sexual violence towards women in South Africa because it does not recognise the links between this and pornography. While the Bill acknowledges that domestic violence is a serious crime against women, and that male violence towards women is an obstacle to achieving gender equality, it fails to understand how pornography disempowers women in the workplace and outside the home, as well as within it. The humiliation women feel when they witness the objectification of another woman generates unimaginable harm, and potentially strips them of the confidence that they can participate in society as leaders. Every time we walk into the newsagents or buy a newspaper at a stall, we are assaulted by pornographic images of women which remind us that we are just bodies and vaginas. Such material constantly reminds women that that they are sexual objects. It is probable that, parallel to this, their male colleagues who imbibe this offensive material sometimes also perceive them as such.

Conclusion

In South Africa, there is no widespread understanding — among the public, among development organisations, in the body of law, or the Bill of Rights — that pornographic imagery is not entertainment or art, but that it denies women their dignity and places them at risk. At times I wonder what would happen if women 'hung a man on a tree and we called it entertainment' (Dworkin 1988).

All forms of violence against women dehumanise us and accentuate our forced subservience to men. I have argued that pornography, like prostitution, ultimately contributes to the image of women as docile objects and men as sex-hungry domineering subjects. Thus, the sexual violence induced by pornography explains why some men find male sexual aggression, and female passivity, erotic and desirable (Russell 1975). It is this preference that often leads men to rape and sexual violence.

It is evident that, according to the available statistics, violence against women in this country are higher than the rest of the world. I have argued that our progressive constitution contributes to this violence and 'rape culture' by legalising the use and sale of pornography, regardless of the harm it inflicts on women. Clearly, the pornography industry both creates and feeds off men's need to control women; the two reinforce and complement each other.

The efforts of both the Government and NGOs in South Africa must be commended. However, to merely concentrate on legislation, providing counselling, and telling women to take care in where they go not solve the problem. In order to complement what these bodies are doing, we must take a closer look at the association between pornography and the increase in the number of rapes and incidence of sexual violence in our society. The Freedom of Speech clause in the Bill of Rights has created a catch-22 situation: it gives with one hand, and takes with the other. This clause is incompatible with the other commitments made in the Bill of Rights regarding equality and non-discrimination, particularly gender equality.

Teboho Maitse is a specialist researcher in the Office of the Status of Women in the Office of the Deputy President, Republic of South Africa. Prior to this she was co-ordinator of the Women's Empowerment Unit, a project of the Speakers' Forum of South Africa, funded by SIDA. She studied for both her MA and PhD at the University of Bradford, UK, and co-convened research on Violence, Abuse, and Gender Relations with Jalna Hamner. She can be contacted via The Editor, Gender and Development.

References

Campbell, C (1992) 'Learning to Kill? Masculinity, The Family and Violence in Natal', Journal of Southern African Studies, Volume 18, Number 3. Pp. 614–628.

CIET Survey, Reconstruct, 6 September 1998, Independent Group, Johannesburg.

Constitution of the Republic of South Africa, 1996, Act 108 of 1996.

Dworkin, A (1988) *Letters from a War Zone (1976–1989)*, New York, EP Dutton.

Hanmer, J (1989) 'Women and Policing in Britain' in Hanmer, J, Radford, J and Stanko, E (eds) *Women, Policing and Male Violence: International Perspectives*, London, Routledge.

Legi-Link Profiles, 20 July 1998, Bill Number B75–88.

Maitse, TE (1997) Women's Experiences of Male Violence Within the Context of the South African National Liberation Struggle, unpublished Ph.D. thesis, University of Bradford, UK.

Russell, DEH (ed) (1993) 'Introduction', in *Making Violence Sexy: Feminist Views on Pornography*, Buckingham, Open University Press.

Russell, D (1975) *The Politics of Rape*, New York, Stein and Day.

Saturday Star, 27 June 1998, Johannesburg: Independent Publishers, page 9.

Spender, D (1982) *Women of Ideas and What Men Have Done to Them*, London: Routledge & Kegan.

Researching 'a family affair':

domestic violence in former Yugoslavia and Albania

Sarah Maguire

In 1998, the author, a feminist lawyer, carried out a research project on behalf of Oxfam GB, studying Bosnia and Hercegovina, Croatia, the Federal Republic of Yugoslavia, and Albania. Maguire discusses the project method and findings, and urges international aid agencies to focus their attention on domestic violence, particularly by working with women's organisations.

In 1997, I was in Sarajevo with a small non-government organisation (NGO), working with displaced women. I and other feminist lawyers of various nationalities (who were also working for Sarajevo-based organisations) decided to set up a local branch of the Lawyers' International Forum for Women's Human Rights. The Forum, of which I am a founder member, had already been active in Bosnia for a year, supporting initiatives to develop legal advice and representation services to women.

The Sarajevo branch of the Forum decided to concentrate on violence against women, as this appeared to be largely ignored by most of the international organisations. Late in 1997, an initial meeting to discuss the issue was held in Sarajevo between members of the Forum, representatives of local women's NGOs, and international organisations, including the International Police Task Force and SFOR (the UN stabilisation force). The group that formed as a result was called the Initiative to Prevent Violence Against Women.

After discussions, members of the Initiative decided not to focus solely on 'domestic' violence (although this later,

perhaps inevitably, became a starting point for much of our work). In contrast, the idea of working on the issue of violence against women in the post-conflict context was immediately popular. It was clear from the interest of those involved in the discussions, and our analysis of the situation in the Balkans, that there was a great deal of work which needed to be done. Some of the local women's organisations had worked specifically on issues of violence against women over the past few years of conflict. Now, working in the aftermath of the worst violence, they were addressing issues including child sexual abuse and domestic violence, through activities including research, advocacy, and counselling.

Starting the work

Many participants already had a good idea of the prevalence of domestic violence in the Sarajevo area, of factors influencing its incidence, and of the response of state and other agencies. However, it was apparent that their work was hampered by the fact that there was no available data on women's experience of violence. In addition, there were areas of work which had not been begun; for example, there was no provision of information for women experiencing violence, and no public awareness campaigns had taken place. Organisations not only lacked the necessary financial resources to carry out such work, they also lacked training. Even in instances where health-care professionals and social workers were receiving training on trauma from international NGOs, very few trainers were able to provide training on gender issues, let alone on violence against women.

Most of the Forum members had worked in Bosnia for some time, and had developed positive relationships with local NGOs. This meant that trust had already been established and the work of the Initiative could proceed more quickly with these organisations. In contrast, the commitment of some of the representatives of international organisations waned after initial enthusiasm, while others were frustrated with not being able to just 'do something' immediately to solve the problem. In my assessment, these problems largely stemmed from organisations' culture. While the police and the army have male-dominated cultures focusing on achieving immediate results, international organisations tended to be uncertain about co-operating with local community organisations on an equal basis and without imposing their own cultural mores. It was clear that the local women's organisations had to take the lead and provide direction, with support from the international community. Those who did continue to meet and work together, did so quite effectively; we seemed able to share our different perspectives and experiences, from Bosnia and the other countries where some of us had worked.

The reaction of international NGOs

News that the Initiative had been formed soon filtered out to international NGOs and inter-governmental organisations. However, international NGOs were not addressing the issue of violence against women in a coherent or concerted manner. In the view of the members of the Initiative, including myself, this indicates a continuing failure on the part of many development workers and policy-makers to recognise that women's rights are human rights.

The obligation to consider violence against women as part of any development strategy is neither merely moral nor simply pragmatic. It is internationally recognised in documents, including the 1995 Beijing Declaration and Platform for Action: 'Violence against women is an obstacle to the achievement of the objectives of equality, development and peace. Violence against women both violates and impairs or nullifies the enjoyment by women of their human rights and fundamental freedoms. The long-standing failure to protect and promote those rights and freedoms in the case of violence against women is a matter of concern to all states, and should be addressed.' (Strategic Objective D, Platform of Action, para. 112, 1995)

The Beijing document goes on to call for action to be taken by governments and non-governmental organisations. It requires that they '(a) provide well-funded shelters and relief support for girls and women subjected to violence, as well as medical, psychological and other counselling services and free or low-cost legal aid, where it is needed...; (b) establish linguistically and culturally accessible services for migrant women and girls,... who are victims of gender-based violence; (c) recognise the vulnerability to violence... of women migrants... (d) support initiatives of women's organisations and non-governmental organisations... to raise awareness on the issue of violence against women and to contribute to its elimination; (e) organise, support and fund community-based education and training campaigns to raise awareness about violence against women as a violation of women's enjoyment of their human rights...; (h) disseminate information on the assistance available to women and families who are victims of violence;' (para. 125).

The continuing refusal on the part of development organisations to participate in these activities confirms the analysis of many feminists working in the area of organisational culture. They conclude that power, in most development organisations, is held by those for whom 'women's issues' are marginal to development. In the context of Bosnia and Hercegovina, such a refusal also shows a failure to recognise that the majority of those displaced in the region are women and children. Lack of understanding of women's experience of violence has led some development agencies to consider that 'psycho-social' work in the post-conflict period is enough to deal with the issue.[1] In fact, violence against women is an ongoing and ubiquitous problem, and a feature of society before, during, and after conflict. The solution to violence against women is prevention; and legal protection, not simply support for victims is required.

Of the international NGOs that heard about the Initiative and were interested in its work, Oxfam GB was unusual in that it had a significant presence in former Yugoslavia, and had a formal commitment to addressing gender issues in the form of its gender policy, agreed in 1993. Despite the fact that Oxfam staff testify to the organisation's relatively limited experience in working on violence against women, (personal commmunication), Oxfam recognises that conflict and crisis affect women disproportionately and differently from men, and has worked and published on this area (El-Bushra and Lopez 1994, Reardon 1994).

This commitment led Oxfam to take a lead on conducting research into the scope and nature of violence against women in the region. Co-operation between Oxfam's

office in Sarajevo, and its advisory Gender and Learning Team at its UK headquarters, meant that an Oxfam-led research project was quickly formulated. Although it did not originate as a request from the Initiative, our members recognised the value of the Oxfam research project and supported it, while I was directly involved as researcher.

The aims of the research

The research was designed to be meet several purposes: first, to indicate whether there was any scope for a programme dealing with violence against women in the region, and then to ascertain what sort of work this would entail; second, to identify potential activities for state bodies, local quangos[2], NGOs, and inter-governmental organisations. The research would also assess how effective Oxfam and other international NGOs were in addressing gender issues, and assess the potential for greater impact. Finally, we hoped that the research would provide an opportunity for advocacy work: by raising the issue with the various agencies, awareness of gender-based violence would be increased, and the topic would gain some legitimacy.

At first, it was planned to confine the research to Bosnia and Hercegovina, but the fact that Oxfam is also present in Croatia, former Yugoslavia, and Albania, and aims to shape its programmes using a wider regional perspective, meant that the research included these countries, too.

The research was designed with the awareness that violence against women includes much more than violence in the home ('domestic violence') — for instance, trafficking, prostitution, and pornography are affecting the lives of women in former Yugoslavia and Albania — but it only looked at 'domestic' violence. It was obvious that a rigorous piece of research covering the wider topic would have taken much more time, and the implementation of a programme coming out of the research would have taken much longer. In addition, we felt that attitudes towards, and lack of adequate provision to deal with, domestic violence are similar to those shown towards violence against women generally. If women are considered dispensable by their husbands, families, and state agencies alike, we can make certain assumptions about attitudes towards selling women to international troops, for instance. We also thought that if women's bodies are on sale in every kiosk and cafe, certain assumptions can be made as to how girls are valued by their boyfriends.

Research methodology

In drawing up the research project, certain areas were identified as of particular relevance for research: the law, legal and other sanctions against perpetrators; legal and other means of protecting women; children facing domestic violence; the role of the international community; and the provision (and potential for provision) of support by local NGOs.

It had been hoped at the outset that I would be able to meet with focus groups of women to discuss their perception of the problem. However, rigorous research into violence against women takes a long time. The subject of domestic violence is so sensitive and so hidden that it is normally impossible to find a group of women who would be prepared to talk about it without a massive amount of preparatory groundwork, including consulting with local women's organisations, advertising through appropriate means, meeting repeatedly to build trust, and providing some form of follow-up support. Moreover, the impact of the war on communities had also added many other difficulties. For example, some women would not want to talk to a woman from their own town for fear of non-confidentiality; they would also feel uncomfortable about talking to a woman

from a community which they think is preventing them from returning home. Primary research would also have to have been conducted in local languages.

Fortunately, some groups had carried out preliminary research which we were able to use, and this confirmed the prevalence of violence and the need for services for women. However, we decided that in follow-up research into the effectiveness of support provided by organisations to women survivors of violence, we should use primary research with women.

I personally interviewed representatives of state agencies at senior and practice levels such as police officers, social workers, judges, health-service staff, lawyers and other legal advisers, members of human-rights organisations and women's organisations, and representatives of the international community, particularly of inter-governmental organisations. Some agencies proved more accessible than others. Police officers and police chiefs were particularly difficult to gain access to, whereas centres for social work were among the easiest of the state institutions. Often, this was due to political considerations and international agencies' reluctance to talk about sensitive issues. More often, it was because interviewees considered the issue of violence against women irrelevant, and/or outside their mandate. In many cases, interviewees' awareness of the issue of violence was increased merely by having to talk about the topic, and consider how their work was failing to address this important aspect of women's lives. The research process demonstrated to local organisations and state institutions that Oxfam has an interest in and commitment to this issue, and to gender issues in general. Women's NGOs and the international community seemed impressed to learn that Oxfam was taking a lead among international organisations in addressing gender-based violence.

The findings

My findings covered each of the four states, detailing the political situation and what impact it has on violence against women. They also dealt with some of wider issues of violence against women, as they intersect with domestic violence. I addressed some theoretical issues, such as the difficulty of defining the terms 'domestic', 'violence', and 'gender violence'.

Failure to learn from gender analyses of conflict and post-conflict situations

A key finding of the research is that gender analyses of women's interests and needs in conflict and post-conflict situations have not been fully taken on by development and relief organisations. Gender analysis of conflict tell us that, during the aftermath of war and in the post-crisis phase of recovery, lives are still seriously disrupted, and that it is women who bear the burden of post-conflict discrimination. For instance, new jobs are given to returning soldiers rather than widows, or women living alone are singled out for harassment by hostile neighbours on ethnic grounds. Further, women tend to be overlooked by agencies providing resources, and they are also traditionally responsible for maintaining family stability, taking care of sick or elderly relatives and children (El-Bushra and Piza Lopez, 1994).

Despite the fact that these points have been well-made in development literature by practitioners as well as academics, I found that these insights had not been translated into action on the part of development and aid agencies in the countries I studied.

Relationship between domestic violence and conflict

One particularly interesting insight from the research is the relationship between the incidence of violence against women in the home and violence in wider society.

Current thinking, previous research, and programmes for action on domestic violence have almost invariably considered the prevalence of domestic violence in the context of a society where there is some degree of stability. In contrast, all the countries surveyed in this research have recently undergone, or are undergoing, intense conflict or crisis.

The occurrence of sexual violence during the war in Bosnia and former Yugoslavia provides a backdrop to the consideration of later, different forms of violence against women and, inevitably, deserves exploration of possible links. In the lead-up to the war in former Yugoslavia, groups providing support to women victims of domestic violence in Belgrade reported that demand for their services increased significantly. The television stations ran propaganda programmes, inflaming nationalism and inciting sentiments of brutality towards particular ethnic groups. The research indicated a consensus among interviewees that notions of male honour, group aggression, and the sovereignty of the nation-state inflamed male violence, as men watching these programmes turned the concomitant aggression and brutality on to their wives and female partners. Women in Belgrade soon learned that the only way to avoid the almost inevitable violence after these programmes was to leave the house (Autonomous Women's Centre Against Sexual Violence, 1996).

However, once the war got underway in Bosnia and Hercegovina, reporting of domestic violence dropped, as evidenced by requests for support to organisations for women victims of violence. Similarly, during the crisis of March 1997 in Albania, women's help-lines reported that the proportion of calls relating to domestic violence dropped dramatically, although the help-line was still busy with calls relating to other matters. It is my contention that if domestic violence actually decreased while men were in the midst of the intense trauma of conflict, or the imme-diate aftermath, this demonstrates that committing domestic violence is a choice, not an inevitability.

One possible explanation, of course, is that women continued to experience the violence, but were simply not reporting domestic violence at a time when their lives and those of their families were under threat from the conflict. However, domestic violence is a life-threatening event, and very few women, if any, call help-lines or seek other help without good reason. This interpretation would wholly underestimate the impact of domestic violence upon the lives of the women who do call in 'normal' circumstances. In addition, the research showed that, once conflict had subsided and 'normality' was restored, women's reports of violence increasing or starting did not relate this to the period of disruption.

To argue that domestic violence is a choice men make is at odds with under-standings of male violence against women which often attribute it to external reasons including men's unemployment or poverty, or to pathological reasons including alco-holism, sickness, or post-traumatic stress disorder. It is undoubtedly true that the disinhibiting effects of alcohol or drugs may have a negative effect upon men's ability or willingness to control their aggression. However, if it is the case that domestic violence actually decreased during the period of conflict, I am forced to conclude that violence is a choice — that men are choosing to inflict violence on the women they purport to love.

Violence and changes in gender roles

Gender analyses of conflict and post-conflict situation have highlighted the danger, once a society is beginning to return to some form of stability (even where this differs markedly from that which it knew before), of a return to what communities believe to be 'traditional' differentiated gender roles. Violence is a way of enforcing women's conformity to such demands (El Bushra and Piza Lopez, 1994). After a conflict, there may be increased stratification of gender roles; in Croatia, where the prohibitions on religious practice that existed during Communism have been lifted, I was given information from women's organisations about the combined pressure women now face from church and state to have more babies and to leave public life.

In some areas, particularly in Bosnia and Hercegovina, almost the entire adult male population were killed, disappeared or fled. Some years after the war, women constitute up to 90 per cent of the popula-tion in some areas. There is little evidence that this is raising women's status and widening their choices, even while it was reported to me that women's expectations of life are growing inversely to men's demands that they return to the home. There is evidence that younger women — who are conscious of the competition to find and keep a man — are tolerating patterns of male behaviour that their older sisters and mothers would have considered unconscionable in pre-war years.

I was told that boys who were 12 or 13 years old when their older brothers and fathers disappeared from the family are now in adolescence. As well as coping with the multi-layered traumas involved in losing all adult men in the family at once and in these circumstances, they are expected (or expect themselves) to adopt the role of senior male family member. Some women's groups reported that this leads to an assumption of the role of batterer, and that these young men, sometimes through an ignorance of any alternative, are using violence against their mothers and sisters in an attempt to assert or to deal with their ascribed authority in this role.

Conclusion

Research is useful, but has obvious limitations if no action follows. It is hoped that our research, along with articles such as this one, will encourage other development agencies and the rest of the international community to accept that women's rights are human rights, that violence against women is a breach of those rights, and that therefore, these organisations have a responsibility to take steps towards combating it.

Those who, during the research, identified priorities for a programme to combat violence against women, echoed the priorities of the Council of Europe's Plan of Action.[3] This document, published in June 1997 with the objective of influencing member states and the European Union as a whole, highlighted the importance of awareness campaigns among the public, abused women, and professionals who deal with women experiencing violence. It also stressed the importance of governments making available resources for support services for women, and for research on the current issues, including the collection of data and official statistics. In additon, there must be a review and reform of legal frameworks addressing violence against women, including violence within marriage and in the home.

I concluded that there is a necessity and a potential for Oxfam to work on this topic, largely carried out through partnerships with local NGOs, and made a series of recommendations. Further research or programme work should be carried out in conjunction with appropriate, autonomous, local women's NGOs, and other community organisations. Where changes have already occurred in prevalence of violence or provision of support, this is due to activism by women and women's groups: they are the most effective and best-informed organisations to do so. In supporting change in this way, international agencies increase their effectiveness, their credibility with the communities in which they work, and, of course, contribute to the reduction in violence against women world-wide.

Sarah Maguire is a practising barrister in London, UK. She is a founder member of the Lawyers' International Forum for Women's Human Rights. Contact details: 14 Tooks Court, Cursitor Street, London EC4A 1LB, UK. E-mail 106363.171@compuserve.com

Notes

1 Support of a practical nature, group therapy, counselling to build self-esteem, and sometimes skills-training may be features of projects in this category.
2 Quango: from 'quasi-NGO', meaning an organisation which, while not entirely independent of the state, has features in common with NGOs.
3 In June 1997, the Council of Europe (comprising member states of the European Union) established a sub-working group to address issues of violence against women.

References

Autonomous Women's Centre Against Sexual Violence, Report, *Violence, Abuse and Women's Citizenship: an International Conference,* Brighton, November 1996.

El Bushra J and Piza Lopez E (1994) *Development and Conflict: the Gender Dimension,* Oxfam, UK.

Howland C (1997) 'The challenge of religious fundamentalism to the liberty and equality rights of women: an analysis under the human rights charter', *Columbia Journal of Transnational Law,* Vol 35 no 2.

Reardon G (1994) *Power and Process: Report from the Women's Linking Project Thailand Conference,* Oxfam, UK.

Interview

Tatyana Lipovskaya, Sisters Sexual Assault Recovery Centre, Moscow, Russia

Please describe the kinds of services 'Sisters' provides for women.

The 'Sisters' Sexual Assault Recovery Centre started in 1993, and the helpline began operating in April 1994. We are an independent not-for-profit organisation, run by women. Counsellors take calls on weekdays from 9am to 9pm. Besides the telephone support, we provide face-to-face counselling (irregularly, in extreme cases, because we do not have a safe place for this kind of activity) and group counselling, including activities such as art therapy. Again, this can only take place if we can find a room to use free of charge.

From the very beginning, we started to work on an educational programme for students focusing on developing a non-violent relationship. There is great demand for such education in schools, colleges, and universities. In 1997, we launched a project aiming to raise awareness of sexual violence among law-enforcement officers. I think this is a very important area of our work, because a devastatingly small number of rape cases in Russia are reported. Women do not trust the police — and for good reason.

The Centre has a long list of agencies which provide services for survivors (medical, legal aid, psychological counselling, employment, and so on). The network of crisis centres and helplines for women in many cities and towns of Russia was established in October 1994.

Who are the women who use the services? What aspects of their lives do you know about?

First, I want to stress that the Centre provides services not only for women — although most of our clients are women, and only women receive face-to-face and group counselling. They are from every strata of Russian society: workers, academics, students, pensioners, artists, housewives, unemployed people — you name it. The help-line received 4,029 crisis calls between 1994-97 — of those, 1,213 were because of sexual violence. In two cases only, the perpetrators of the violence were women. Men suffered sexual violence in 67 cases; the rest were women. The age of the victims ranged from two-and-a-half years old, to 92 — this was an old man who was suffering domestic violence. Most of the perpetrators of sexual violence were not strangers — just like everywhere else in the world. In 1997, of 357 cases, 196 offenders were husbands, friends, fathers and stepfathers, grandfathers, schoolmates, partners, neighbours, teachers, cousins, brothers, uncles, and bosses — you see, there's no safe place!

The overwhelming number of clients call only once; they get support in the form of referral and other information, and never call again. Our clients usually want to get information about medical services (we have a long list of clinics, hospitals, and medical centres), or legal aid (in this sphere we can only put them in touch with either volunteer lawyers or commercial legal services). Often, women ask us about employment — where can they find a job? Other questions are about other crisis centres specialising in domestic violence, HIV/AIDs, alcoholism, and drug abuse.

We don't get to know very much about most callers' lives. However, sometimes a caller tells us all about her life for 40 to 50 minutes, and then the counsellor gets a rather fuller picture. It is easier, however, to know a person better if she is a 'regular' client — we have a dozen such clients. Then you get to know her family status, her occupation, her hobbies, friends and enemies, her bright days, and her dark ones. The most effective strategy is, of course, face-to-face counselling, when women become really close, help each other and trust each other completely. It is the most rewarding relationship — though very hard work on both sides.

How has the economic and political transition in Russia affected the lives of your clients? Do you think the kinds of violence they experience has got worse since the end of communism?

As you can easily guess, the economic changes affect the lives of every member of society, especially, I believe, the lives of women. A phrase which our media seem to repeat *ad nauseam* is 'unemployment in Russia has a woman's face'. I don't think that the kinds of violence have got worse, perhaps they have become more widespread and affect a greater number of women. Also, women have become more vulnerable; probably this has happened to some men who suffer violence, too. We get calls from men who are victims of domestic violence, sexual harrassment at work from both male and female bosses, and rape (the rapists are other men). I think male rape is a big problem, especially bearing in mind the violation of men's human rights in the army. Our Centre, however, does receive many more calls from women, and women's liberation is my own big interest. Now, we have this novelty, 'new Russians': very rich relatively young or middle-aged men. Their wives are sometimes our clients. Perhaps this is a distinctive feature of 'post-communism'.

Although it's not the topic of this interview, I would like to add that children are obviously most vulnerable, and they suffer all kinds of violence everywhere. On the other hand, their protection is guaranteed by the law. Society is inclined to pay more attention to children than to women. In Moscow, there are a number of organisations whose goal is children's well-being: help-lines, medical centres, centres for children with special needs, orphanages, and shelters. I think violence against children in Russia is a tremendous problem, but the issue is very painful for me, and I am not an expert in this sphere.

One other significant aspect is that after the fall of communism, Russian society in general now speaks more openly about all kinds of violence — from different points of view.

What do you think is the best thing about the Sisters project? And what would you like to improve in future?

When we started our Centre, I was so excited to have an opportunity to apply my beliefs and principles to this project; all co-founders were committed to the philosophy of equality and having a non-hierarchical structure for the organisation. Certainly, it is good that the Centre is a not-for-profit organisation, and that we provide services to everybody regardless of their age, sex, occupation, sexual orientation, and so on. It was very inspiring to have the support and attention of every member of the group.

For the future, sure, we would like to have more respect and support from authorities. We are keen to educate police officers to make them more sensitive regarding the issue of violence against women. One great improvement I am dreaming of is to have a 'room of one's own': I'd like to have a counselling centre with a multi-channel helpline, rooms for individual and group counselling, a resource centre, a creche, and so on.

What kind of difficulties does the Sisters project face for its future work?

From the beginning, and now too, our main problem has been finance and the absence of any cheap place for the office, money to fund the helpline, and so on. We cannot solve this without outside help. To date, the Centre has received no material support of any kind from the Russian authorities. All our funds have been provided by Western foundations, organisations, and individuals. Every year the Centre has to seek funds to survive — which does not help us to feel stable and confident about the future.

I think that, as a result of the efforts of women's NGOs, the government in Russia is slowly and reluctantly beginning to admit the existence of 'women's issues', and that rape and domestic violence is a big social problem, not a private matter. Since 1996, women activists — NGO members, MPs, lawyers, and so on — have been lobbying to bring in a law on domestic violence. After 24 hearings, it has not yet been passed. When I speak to people in authority, especially women, they seem to sympathise with our work, nodding in sorrow, expressing deep regret, some of them even promising to help...but in Moscow, we still don't have a single shelter for women victims of domestic violence, and we don't have inexpensive, convenient locations for crisis centres. And institutions like the police include staff who contribute to the problem. One woman reported to the police that she had been gang-raped. The officer who was receiving her written statement said: 'You're unclean already

then, so it would not do any harm if I have sexual intercourse with you. I will register your claim after that'. The woman submitted.

I want to draw your attention to the fact that life in Moscow and St Petersburg differs dramatically from life in small towns and villages in Russia and other republics of the Russian Federation. I don't know much about the situation in these places. There is a town in northern Russia called Langepas where women are very active and receive a lot of support from the local authorities; Ekaterinburg, a big industrial city in the Urals, can be proud of its developed network of crisis centres and psychological support for women. Yet there are other places like Voronezh, a town to the south of Moscow, where a friend of mine is struggling hard, almost single-handedly, to create a crisis centre for women.

You can see, we are not helpless or hopeless. I cannot say for sure, but I think we will be able to make the state take some measures to improve women's situation.

Do you think there are elements of Russian culture, past or present, which condone violence against women?

It's a big question, isn't it? I think Russia's notorious gender stereotypes are now even stronger. Russian women in the past have had an image of being very strong and independent, but according to Russian traditions they were obliged to show respect and submit to men — fathers, brothers, and husbands. One could recite many Russian proverbs which degrade and humiliate women: 'Hen is not a bird, women is not a human being'; 'Long hair — empty brain'; and so on. And what about the widespread belief that 'if he beats me, he loves me'?

Nowadays, in the period of economic and political transition, both women and men have to fight to keep their jobs, but this affects women worse because of beliefs that they should stay at home to play the role of mother and housekeeper. On the other hand, many women are tired of earning money for many years by doing tedious, hard work; they are happy to be at home. They now see it as their husbands' duty to earn money and guarantee the family's well-being. So far, so good. But there are not many well-paid jobs to support this lifestyle, so women and men both get frustrated, annoyed, depressed, and enraged. This kind of situation triggers domestic violence. At the other extreme, violence flourishes as well. Let's take the so-called 'New Russians', who are rich men who consider themselves the masters of life. They are sure that everything belongs to them: money, cars, houses, land, and women (especially women's bodies). Their attitude is: *What? Women do not want them? Nonsense! Do they dare to fight back? OK, they've asked for it!* And so on.

How did you become involved in the Sisters project? What is your professional and personal background?

I was born on a train and spent my first four years north of the Arctic circle, in Vorkuta, and then in the Russian south in the oil town of Maikop. After high school I worked as a typist, a hydrogeologist, a computer operator, journalist, translator, and a counsellor. I have been actively involved in the women's movement for the last ten years. Since 1993 I have been closely involved in setting up the Sisters Centre in Moscow; since 1997 I have been chairperson of the board of directors, and work as a volunteer on the help-line.

Tatyana Lipovskaya can be contacted at Sisters, PO Box 38, 113035 Moscow, Russia. Fax/tel: +70 (95) 112 3129

Resources

Compiled by Emma Bell

Books and videos

Embodied Violence: Communalising Women's Sexuality in South Asia, Kumari Jayawardena and Malathi DeAlwis (eds.), Zed Books, 1996. This book examines the way in which societies play out the struggle for cultural identities on women's bodies. It covers the relationship between motherhood, tradition, community, racial purity and how women's bodies are used as the surface for repressive cultural practices and symbolic humiliations.

Femicide: The politics of Women Killing Jill Radford and Diana E H Russell (eds.), Open University Press, 1992. Over 40 contributors explore femicide across nations and cultures and assess the role of social values and institutions in perpetuating it. Contributors also suggest action to combat different forms of femicide.

Gender and Catastrophes, Ronit Lentin (ed.), Zed Books, 1997. Explores gendered and gendering effects of violence against women in war and other disasters, and the way in which women are targeted in extreme situations such as war, genocide, famines, slavery, mass rape, and ethnic cleansing. Country- and culture-specific examples include Tibet's reproductive policy, nuclear testing in the Pacific, the Holocaust, 'comfort women' in World War Two, and women's coerced participation and genocidal rape in the Rwandan massacres.

Gender Violence: Interdisciplinary Perspectives, L I O'Toole, JR Schiffman (eds.), New York University Press, 1997. An anthology of central articles and authors plus original pieces about gender violence, from a wide range of disciplines. Examines the roots of male violence and the victimisation of women, explores forms of sexual coercion and violence, and includes a number of perspectives on promoting non-violent gender relations. Essays explore sexual harassment, rape, child abuse, battering in intimate relationships, and pornography.

Justice through the Eyes of Women, Court of Women — Testimonies on Violence against Women in the Arab World Beirut, Lebanon, 28–30 June 1995. Highlights major testimonies and the declaration from the 'Court of Women', held in June 1995 in Beirut, Lebanon. Women from 14 Arab countries participated in this event. Creative symbolism and testimonies combine to expose and bring to trial the various forms of violence perpetrated against Arab women. For more information about the book, write to: El Taller, BP 137 1002, Tunis-Belvedere, Tunisia, E-mail: eltaller@gn.apc.org

Mass Rape: The War against Women in Bosnia-Herzegovina, A Stiglmayer (ed.), University of Nebraska Press, 1994. Testimonies of women who have endured rape and lost loved ones. The essays also address the human rights of women and children and how the women's movement has reacted to the atrocities in former Yugoslavia.

What Women do in Wartime: Gender and Conflict in Africa, Meredeth Turshen and Clotilde Twagiramariya (eds.), Zed Books, 1993.
The first book to examine rape and other forms of gendered political violence in African civil wars, this book is also about women taking action for change. A mixture of reportage, testimony and scholarship, it includes contributions from women in Chad, Liberia, Mozambique, Namibia, Rwanda, South Africa, and Sudan.

A Modern Form of Slavery: Trafficking of Burmese Women and Girls into Brothels in Thailand, Asia Watch and Women's Rights Project, 1993.
Thousands of Burmese women and girls are trafficked into Thai brothels every year, where they work under conditions tantamount to slavery. Those who control the trafficking (including police and border officials) routinely escape punishment. *A Modern Form of Slavery* is based on interviews with victims and documents the violation of their rights. It also presents recommendations to governments and the international community for protecting the rights of women and girls and prosecuting their abusers.

No Safe Haven: Male Violence against Women at Home, at Work and in The Community, M P Koss, L A Goodman, A Browne, American Psychological Association, Washington DC, 1994.
Informs about violence faced by women in the USA, such as crimes against women, abuse, conjugal violence, sexual harassment, and rape.

The Violences of Men, Jeff Hearn, Sage Publications, London, 1998.
From a pro-feminist perspective, Hearn critically assesses the theoretical frameworks which are used to explain male violence. Drawing on extensive original research, he addresses the issue of men's violence against women whom they know within the wider context of men's use of power and violence in society.

The Public Nature of Private Violence: The Discovery of Domestic Abuse, R Mykituik, and M Albertson Fineman (eds.), Routledge, 1994.
A wide range of topics on domestic violence: personal narratives, local legislation, and international human-rights law. Includes studies from Canada and Ghana, and explores issues such as child abuse, incest, violence in lesbian relationships, non-physical violence, and state-sanctioned violence. Violence is placed in its social and cultural context.

Rape for Profit: Trafficking of Nepali Girls and Women to India's Brothels, Human Rights Watch/Asia, 1995.
Draws links between political and economic situations and patterns of abuse. Documents how women are recruited and their working conditions. Also examines the role of the Nepal and Indian governments, their corruption, complicity, and denial of the ongoing abuse of girls and women from Nepal. Other relevant issues considered are health care, birth control, and HIV/Aids.

Rape Warfare: The Hidden Genocide in Bosnia-Herzegovina and Croatia, B Allen, University of Minnesota Press, 1996.
This book gives the history of the mass femicide and genocidal campaign by Serbian forces against the people of Bosnia-Herzegovina and Croatia. The rape and murder of women was not an unintended consequence of war, but a strategy of systematic terror devised by the Serb leaders before the fighting began. Includes survivors' accounts of the death/rape camps and interviews with people who have tried to help those affected.

Stolen Lives: Trading Women into Sex and Slavery, Sietske Altink, Scarlet Press (London) and Harrington Park Press (New York), 1995.
Examines how women are hired in their home country, transported, left without money, passports or permits, and how they become trapped in prostitution and domestic slavery. Includes women's testimonies, explores international crime networks which exploit women, and exposes the lack of action at the regional, national, and international levels.

Cutting the Rose: Female Genital Mutilation: The Practice and its Prevention, Efua Dorkenoo, Minority Rights Publication, 1994.
This classic book discusses female genital mutilation (FGM), health and human rights

issues arising from it, and international initiatives to end the practice. It includes some case studies from Africa, explores the practice in Western countries, and discusses strategies for prevention. This book brings together accounts of attempts by the UN, WHO, and NGOs to tackle this issue, and makes suggestions to build on existing strategies to end FGM at all levels.

Warrior Marks: Female Genital Mutilation and the Sexual Blinding of Women, Alice Walker and Pratibha Parmar, 1993.
This is an account of the writers' personal exploration of the practice of female circumcision for a documentary of the same name. During their fieldwork they gathered a range of testimonies from supporters and opponents of FGM. Walker and Parmar include personal accounts from women and girls who have undergone the practice. This book is difficult to get hold of outside the USA. It is available in the UK from FORWARD, 40 Eastbourne Terrace, London W2 3RQ, UK.

Women and Prostitution, V Bullough, B Bullough, Prometheus Books, 1993.
Explores the historical, sociological, and anthropological background of prostitution. It covers many cultural dilemmas such as women as property, pornography, fear of sexuality, religion, promiscuity, sex and social class, and control of venereal disease.

Women and Violence: Realities and Responses Worldwide, Miranda Davies (ed), Zed Books, 1994.
This collection documents the experiences and analyses of individual women and groups from over 30 countries as diverse as Papua New Guinea, Argentina, Tanzania, Scotland, France, Bosnia, India, and Tibet. Essays examine domestic violence, child sexual abuse, sexual harassment in the workplace, rape and torture in war, genital mutilation, and the effect of men's violence on women's reproductive health. Contributors attest to the wealth of activities generated by grassroots women's organisations throughout the world.

Women's Rights, Human Rights: International Feminist Perspectives, Julie Peters and Andrea Wolpier (Eds.), Routledge, 1994.
A collection of contributions from activists, journalists, lawyers, and scholars from 21 countries. They address such topics as rape as a war crime in former Yugoslavia, domestic violence, international human rights law, trafficking of women, FGM, women's reproductive rights, and the persecution of lesbians.

Women in a Violent World: Feminist Analysis and Resistance across Europe, Chris Corrin (ed.) Edinburgh University Press, 1996.
Explores the commonalities and differences experienced by female victims of male violence across race, class, religion, sexual orientation, and nationality in Russia, Hungary, Ireland, Belgrade, Croatia, Spain, and the UK. Also considers how women resist oppression even in times of severe crisis, and explores feminist analyses of such experiences.

Women's Encounters with Violence: Australian Experiences, Judith Bessant (ed), Sage Series on Violence Against Women, 1997.
Gives the history of violence against women in Australia and explains how culturally embedded laws and customs perpetuate women's oppression. Culturally specific examples include violence within the Aboriginal community and in the Torres Strait Islands. Issues that cross cultural boundaries, such as violence against women with disabilities, homeless women, and violence in lesbian relationships are also considered.

Women, Violence and Male Power: Feminist Activism in Research and Practice, M Hester, L Kelly, J Radford, Open University Press, 1996.
A collection of developments, ideas, and discussions arising from the work of the British Sociological Association of Violence against Women Study Group. Contributors examine the issues and questions that are central to our understanding of sexual violence and abuse, as well as the development of the latest research in this area. Also documents different women's experiences and ways of coping with male violence.

Women Violence and Social Change,
R E Dobash and R P Dobash, Routledge, 1992.
Comparative study of British and American responses to the problem of violence against women. Show how feminist activists created an international social movement, and describes the ensuing response of the state, justice system, therapeutic professions, and academic research in each country.

Rethinking Violence against Women, R E Dobash and R P Dobash, (eds.), Routledge, 1998.
This book opens for discussion and debate key issues around the nature and causes of violence against women, across a variety of disciplines which, in the editors' view, might otherwise not meet. The purpose is not to convert the proponents of one approach to another, but to introduce the ideas, evidence, and concerns of each to the other in the hope that such cross-fertilisation will lead to innovation and enhance all the approaches.

Women and War, J Vickers, Zed Books, 1993.
Explores the relationship between the condition of women and all forms of aggression. Uses data to show that the oppression of women contributes to and is a consequence of war.

Our Bodies, Ourselves for the New Century,
Marianne Winters et al., Touchstone (a division of Simon and Schuster Inc), 1998.
This completely updated edition of the famous self-help manual includes a comprehensive section on violence against women. Aspects covered which relate to violence against women are race, class, blaming the victim, sexual harassment, domestic violence, incest and sexual abuse of children, the sex industry, and defending ourselves against violence. For more details contact http:///www.feminist.com

Sisters and Daughters Betrayed.
A video about the realities of sex trafficking and forced prostitution released in 1995 by independent video-maker Chela Blitt. Examines the economics of trafficking and the parallels between the situation in Asia and other regions. It presents interviews with activist women in Asia who are involved in campaigns against trafficking. Send US $8 to:

The Global Fund for Women, 425 Sherman Avenue, Suite 300, Palo Alto, CA 94306, USA.

Organisations

Europe

Association Européenne Contre les Violences Faites aux Femmes au Travail (AVFT), 71 rue St Jacques, 75005 Paris, France.
Offers a list of resources concerning violence against women.

Be Active Be Empowered (B.a.B.e.), Petreciecev Trg 3, 41000 Zagreb, Tel/fax: +385 (41) 419 302, E-mail: babe_zg@zamir-zg.ztn.apc.org
B.a.B.e. is engaged in project-oriented activities such as education on women's human rights; rights of women refugees, migrants, and asylum seekers; women's political rights campaigns; positive images of women in the media; providing free legal advice; lobbying and monitoring legal practices; and changing Croatia's discriminatory laws.

British Council, The Gender Team, UK Partnerships, Bridgwater House, 58 Whitworth Street, Manchester M1 6BB, UK. Published a Network Newsletter (March 1998) on Violence against Women. Development and Gender web site: http://www.britcoun.org/social/

Centre for Women War Victims, Dordiceva 6, 41000 Zagreb, Tel: +385 (41) 434 189, Fax +385 (41) 433 416, E-mail: cenzena_zg@zamir-zg.ztn.apc.org

Women's Aid Federation of England (there are also federations in Wales, Scotland, and Northern Ireland), PO Box 391, Bristol BS99 7WS, UK, Tel: +44 (117) 944 4411, Fax: +44 (117) 942 1703, E-mail wafe@wafe.co.uk.
Organises campaigns and provides services for women and children escaping domestic violence. Also has a connection with a Bulgarian organisation : Animus Association, PO Box 97, 1408 Sofia, Bulgaria.

WOMANKIND World-wide, 3 Albion Place, Galena Road, Hammersmith, London W6 0LT, UK, Tel: +44 (181) 563 8607, E-mail: womankind@gn.apc.org

http://www.oneworld.org/womankind
Supports projects worldwide to combat violence against women.

Women Living Under Muslim Law (WLML), Bôite Postale 23, 34790 Grabels, (Montpellier), France.
WLML provide an excellent list of resources on different forms of violence faced by women, particularly those living in Muslim societies.

Asia
Tibetan Woman's Association,
http://www.grannyg.bc.ca/tibet/tibet.html
A non-government organisation based in Dharamsala, India with over 37 branches in India and abroad. Amongst the major concerns of the organisation is the violation of Tibetan women's rights.

Global Alliance against Trafficking in Women (GAATW), The International Co-ordination Office, PO Box 1281, Bangrak Post Office, Bangkok 10500, Thailand, Tel: +662 864 1427 8, Fax: +662 864 1637.
http://www.inet.co.th/org/gaatw/updated.htm
An international alliance for better co-ordination of national and global action.

Association of Women for Action and Research, Block 5, Dover Crescent #01-22, Singapore 13 000 5, Tel: +65 779 7137, Fax: +65 777 0318.
Runs a small documentation centre and has published some booklets on domestic violence.

British Council Division in Calcutta, 5 Shakespeare Sarani, Calcutta 700 071, India, Tel: +91 (33) 2855370/2825378/2823445.
Conducted a regional workshop on women against violence in March 1998. Information available on participants and papers presented.

Forum against the Oppression of Women, 120 Safalya Building, 1st Floor, Currey Road, N M Joshi Marg, Bombay 400012, India.
Formed in 1979 as a platform to respond to an extremely unjust judgement on a rape case. Committed to supporting women's groups working on controversial and difficult issues.

Gabriela Commission on Violence against Women, 20-B Florina Street, Roxas District, Quezon City, Philippines.

War Against Rape (WAR), 102 Pearl Crest, 18-C 4th Commercial Lane, Zamzama Boulevard, D.H.A. Phase V, Karachi 75500, Pakistan, Tel: +92 (21) 57 3008.
http://www.rpi.edu/~ashrafs/war.html
With chapters in Karachi and Lahore, WAR is dedicated to combating sexual crimes against women. Activities include providing legal, medical, psychological, and moral support to victims of rape; creating awareness about violent crimes against women; and keeping up the pressure on Government and law enforcement agencies to prevent such crimes and improve the handling of criminal cases.

Women's Aid Organisation, Pertubuhan Wanita, PO Box 493, Jalan Sultan, 46760 Petaling Jaya, Selangor Darul Ehsan, Malaysia.
Provides information about action taken in Malaysia to combat violence against women.

Latin America
Belize Women against Violence Movement, PO Box 1190, Belize City, Belize.

Caribbean Association for Feminist Research and Action (CAFRA), PO Box 442, Tunapuna Post Office, Trinidad and Tobago, West Indies.
CAFRA, in collaboration with UNIFEM, is implementing a regional tribunal on violence against women, among other activities. E-mail: cafrainfo@wow.net for a list of references on women and violence available.

Colectivo de Lucha Contra la Violencia hacia las Mujeres, Santa Ma. La Ribera 107-8, Col. Santa Ma. La Ribera, 06400 Mexico City, Mexico.

Violence, Health and Development Project, Apartado Postal 471-1011, San Jose, Costa Rica.

North America
Center for Women's Global Leadership, Douglas College, Rutgers University, 27 Clifton Avenue, New Brunswick, NJ 08903, USA, Tel: +1 (732) 932 8782, Fax: +1 (732) 932 1180, E-mail: cwgl@igc.apc.org
Campaigns and has a range of resources on all forms of violence against women.

The Global Fund for Women
425 Sherman Avenue, Suite 300,

Palo Alto, California 94306-1823, USA,
Tel: +1 (650) 853-8305, Fax: +1 (650) 328-0384,
E-mail: gfw@globalfundforwomen.org
http://www.igc.apc.org/gfw/
An international organisation that focuses on women's human rights and provides grants for groups which work for women's well-being and full participation in society.

International League for Human Rights, 432 Park Avenue South, New York, NY 10016, USA, Tel: +1 (212) 684 1221, Fax: +1 (212) 684 1696. Report of a conference sponsored in collaboration with the international Women's Rights Action Watch, Combating Violence against Women, available from the above address.

RAINBO, 915 Broadway, Suite 1109, New York, NY 10010-7108, USA, Fax: +1 (212) 477 4154. http://www.rainbo.org/
A not-for-profit organisation working on the links between health and human rights, emphasising every woman's right to reproductive and sexual health. While contributing to the advancement of the field in general, RAINBO is currently focusing on FGM.

Status of Women Canada, 350 Albert Street, 5th Floor, Ottawa, Ontario, KIA IA3, Canada. Has a wealth of resources concerning violence faced by women in Canada and information about strategies for change.

The Women's Human Rights Program, Amnesty International, 322 8th Avenue, New York, NY 10001, USA, E-mail: whrprogram@aiusa.org http://www.amnesty-usa.org/women/
Promotes women's human rights within Amnesty's mandate. It seeks to stop the particular violations of civil and political rights that women and girls experience. The web site currently has information about women in Afghanistan.

World Council of Muslim Women Foundation, Contact Dr. Fahlman, PO 128, Seba Beach, Alberta T0E 2B0, Canada, Tel/Fax: +1 (403) 439 5088, E-mail: wcomwf@connect.ab.ca
A global not-for-profit organisation dedicated to the education and safety of all women.

Africa
Comité National de Lutte Contre les Violences Faites aux Femmes, C/o RADI, BP 12085, Dakar, Senegal, Tel: +221 824 60 48, Fax: 825 75 36.

Groupe de Recherche Femmes et Lois au Senegal (Grefels), BP 5339, Dakar, Senegal, Tel/Fax: +221 825 65 33.

Musasa Project, PO Box A205, Avondale, Harare, Zimbabwe.
Organisation working on supporting women survivors of violence, popular education on violence, advocacy for changing legal systems, and training staff of legal institutions.

Sister Collective,
PO Box 60100, Katutura, 9000 Namibia.

National Network on Violence against Women (South Africa), Mmabatho Ramagoshi, National Office, P O Box 72957, Lynwood Ridge 0040, Pretoria, South Africa, Tel: +27 (12) 348 1233.
An independent body comprising representatives of provincial networks and national government departments, and other relevant bodies. The Network is an autonomous, voluntary association whose main purpose is the eradication of violence against women.

Campaigns

25 November was designated as the Day of Non-violence against Women at the first Latin American and Caribbean Feminist Conference in 1981. Subsequently, this was expanded to '16 Days of Action' to link 25 November with International Human Rights Day on 10 December. For information contact the Center for Women's Global Leadership (See above, under Organisations, North America).

United Nations Development Fund for Women (UNIFEM)
The United Nations has dedicated the period 25 November 1997–10 December 1998 to Women's Human Rights and the theme 'A Life Free of Violence'. UNIFEM is

co-ordinating activities for this period. Tel: +1 (246) 437 3970/1/2, Fax: +1 (246) 437 7674 for further information about campaigns. See below for web site details.

Web Sites

Q Web Sweden
http:www.qweb.kvinnoforum.se/qabout.htm
A global communication network for exchange of experience and ideas on women's health and gender issues. They have recently started an anti-trafficking project, which is profiled on this site, and also provide an extensive resource base of information on violence and abuse.

Abuse Against Women
http://www.alternatives.com/libs/womabuse.htm
Small database of text documents focusing on abuse, sex abuse, workplace harassment, and rape. Mostly North American but includes some developing country content, too.

Mining Company
http://women3rdworld.miningco.com/
An excellent web site containing news, organisations, resources, and articles on a variety of issues faced by women in developing countries, including violence against women.

International Centre for Human Rights and Democratic Development
http://www.ichrdd.ca/PublicationsE/biblioWomen.html
Comprehensive list of resources about women in conflict situations.

Feminist Majority Foundation
http://feminist.com/violence.htm
This site collects dozens of resources on domestic violence, rape, and violence against women, child sexual abuse, female genital mutilation and sexual harassment. Mainly information about resources in the USA.

Women's Net
http://www.igc.org/igc/womensnet
Information about violence against women worldwide.

Women's Net South Africa
http://womensnet.org.za/pvaw/vaw.htm
Lists campaigns and organisations, and outlines the understanding of violence against women in South Africa. Internet links to African and international organisations.

UNIFEM
http://www.unifem.undp.org/csw98.htm
Information about international resolutions concerning violence against women, UNIFEM's work, and resources available.
unifem.undp.org/trust.htm
Information about Trust Fund in support of action to eliminate violence against women.

Female Genital Mutilation Research Home Page
http://www.hollyfields.org/~fgm/

Conference on Family Violence
http://www.wcfv.org
Details on a conference held in Singapore, September 1998, organised by a variety of organisations including the United Nations.

South Asian Women
http://www.umiacs.umd.edu/users/sawweb/sawnet/violence
Information about domestic violence in South Asia and organisations that can offer help. Links to similar worldwide resources.

Coalition against Trafficking in Women
http://www.uri.edu/artsci/wms/hughes/catw

Oneworld
http://www.oneworld.org/guides/women/violence.html
Information about women and conflict, and links to women's anti-war organisations in former Yugoslavia.

Australian Institute for Women's Research and Policy
http://www.gu.edu.au/gwis/aiwrap/AIWRAP.home.html
The first gender-issues research centre in Australia to focus on the links between academics, government, industry, and the wider community in the development of policies affecting women and gender issues. AIWRAP aims to create a dialogue between women's issues researchers and policy practitioners, in

private enterprise, the government, and the community. Through this dialogue, AIWRAP aims to provide research expertise to enhance the status of women in Australian society.

Journals and Reports

Violence against Women is a journal dedicated to the dissemination of original research and scholarship on all aspects of violence against women, including sexual assault and coercion, sexual harassment, female infanticide, domestic violence, and incest. For subscription rates, contact Journals Subscriptions Manager, SAGE Publications Ltd, 6 Bonhill Street, London, EC2A 4PU, UK, Fax: +44 (171) 374 8741, Credit Card Hotline +44 (171) 330 1266.

Violence and Abuse Abstracts,
Sage Publications, 2455 Teller Road,
Thousand Oaks, CA 91320, USA,
or 6 Bonhill Street, London EC2A 4PU, UK.

Women's Studies International Forum,
Elsevier Science Inc., 660 White Plain Road, Tarrytown, New York, 10591-5133, USA, E-mail: ESUK.USA@ELSEVIER.COM or The Boulevard, Langford Lane, Kidlington, Oxford, OX5 1GB, UK.
Bi-monthly journal to aid the distribution and exchange of feminist research in international women's studies and other fields. It does not deal explicitly with violence against women, but includes many articles on the topic.

Gender Violence: A Development and Human Rights Issue, C Bunch and R Carrillo, Dublin, Attic Press 1992 (Pamphlet).

Mainly looking at violence against women in Ireland. Available from the Center for Women's Global Leadership (See above, under Organisations, North America).

Untold Terror: Violence against Women in Peru's Armed Conflict, Report by Americas Watch and the Women's Rights Project, 1992. For information about this and other publications by Women's Rights Project contact: Women's Rights Project, 152K Street NW, Suite 910, Washington DC 20005, USA.

Russia: Too Little, Too Late: State Response to Violence against Women , Human Rights Watch Report, New York, 1998.
Report on the pervasive problem of violence against women in Russia.

South Africa: Violence Against Women and the Medico-Legal System , Human Rights Watch Report, New York, 1997.
Examines the state's response to violence against women, recent developments in government policy, the system's continuing failure to respond to violence against women, and the role of the South African health-care system in combating violence against women.

For a list of other publications by Human Rights Watch or to order the above contact: Human Rights Watch, Publications Department, 485 Fifth Avenue, New York 10017-6104, USA, E-mail: hrwnyc@hrw.org

Voices of Resistance, Silences of Pain:
A Resource Guide on Violence Against Women,
Vyas, Anju et al, Centre for Women's Development Studies, New Delhi, 1996.

Index to Volume 6